CLOSE TO
THE WIND

CLOSE TO THE WIND

The Autobiography of Britain's
Greatest Olympic Sailor

Ben Ainslie

With Nick Townsend

YELLOW JERSEY PRESS
LONDON

Published by Yellow Jersey Press 2009

4 6 8 10 9 7 5 3

Copyright © Ben Ainslie 2009

Ben Ainslie has asserted his right under the Copyright, Designs and
Patents Act 1988 to be identified as the author of this work

First published in Great Britain in 2009 by
Yellow Jersey Press
Random House, 20 Vauxhall Bridge Road,
London SW1V 2SA

www.rbooks.co.uk

Addresses for companies within The Random House Group Limited can be found at:
www.randomhouse.co.uk/offices.htm

The Random House Group Limited Reg. No. 954009

A CIP catalogue record for this book
is available from the British Library

ISBN 9780224082921

The Random House Group Limited supports The Forest Stewardship Council (FSC),
the leading international forest certification organisation. All our titles that are
printed on Greenpeace approved FSC certified paper carry the FSC logo.
Our paper procurement policy can be found at:
www.rbooks.co.uk/environment

Typeset by SX Composing DTP, Rayleigh, Essex
Printed and bound in Great Britain by
CPI Mackays, Chatham ME5 8TD

To my family, for all their love and support

Contents

List of Illustrations

Chapter 1

Golden Ambitions

For four years I'd waited for this moment. As I readied my boat and set out for the start line, my mind was attuned, not just to an assault on gold, but to the opportunity to defeat my arch-rival Robert Scheidt.

Destiny had decreed that on 29 September 2000, the final race at the Sydney Olympics would be a climactic contest between myself and the brilliant Brazilian. The waters of Sydney Harbour were to be the setting for a compelling duel between two of the world's most committed sailors. It was the classic sporting confrontation. Anticipation gripped those watching.

It was a race for gold, but it was also a vengeance match. We had first encountered each other four years before, at the 1996 Atlanta Olympics, when I had been just 19 years old. There Scheidt had got the better of me in the final race of the series. He had claimed gold, leaving me with the consolation of a silver.

The Brazilian is four years my senior, and I had been aware of his reputation as one of the world's most fiercely competitive sailors well before then. When I first came into the class in Atlanta, he was initially very supportive. Every so often he'd sail past, and say 'Maybe you could try this, or that.' That soon changed when I started being a threat to him. Since our final race showdown in 1996 I had known that this was the man I'd have to beat if I ever wanted to win anything.

Now, in Sydney, I had my chance to do so. It called for composure and radical thinking. After a week's racing, the situation boiled down to this: in the finale of the series I had to either go out and beat Robert by at least ten places to win the gold, or, because of the intricacies of the discard system (at that time you could discount your two worst results), if I could sail him down the fleet and ensure that he finished no better than twenty-first, he'd have to count that as one of his discarded races, and that would give me the gold.

Because the conditions were so shifty, I couldn't take a chance with the former. I spoke to my then coach, John Derbyshire, who, I should stress, is normally a calm and non-confrontational kind of character. I already had it in my mind what I had planned. I said 'John, these conditions are so crazy, if I go out and try to win the race, it's in God's hands. The only way I can make sure I win is by sailing him down the fleet.' In other words, my tactics would purely concentrate on ensuring Robert finished at the back of the field.

John wasn't sure. He replied: 'If you're going to do that, you've got to make sure you really do a good job and hammer the guy.' He added: 'You can't just give him a hard time at the start. You've got to put him so far back, he hasn't got a chance.' We decided on the tactics. There was something inside me that really relished the challenge of carrying them out. It was a tough ask to carry out successfully what we had in mind. But if I could pull it off, it'd be an amazing feat against such a talented sailor.

Robert's a very professional sportsman, incredibly fit, highly motivated and extremely well prepared. There was a certain element of him being the big guy in the fleet, deserving respect from all his rivals, and trying to use that as a force to try and gain an advantage on the water. He had instilled a belief in other Laser sailors that he was unbeatable. I refused to subscribe to that but I also retained the utmost respect for him. He could be temperamental on the water, though nothing like one particular individual I will mention later. We're both very similar. We never give in. Right until the end of our races against each other, we pushed each other to the limit.

He'd won the world championships of 1997, but gradually I'd begun to gain the upper hand. I'd captured the 1998 and 1999 world championships, and defeated Scheidt in the process. He came back to beat me in 2000, and his form going into Sydney was actually better than mine.

Normally, Olympic racing is out to sea, and the wind, light or strong, is relatively steady. Sydney was a very different venue. Its waters, usually a beautiful backdrop for people to go about their business, and in which small boats bob around picturesquely, created an environment I got to know well in the build-up to the Olympics.

The topography of the surrounding land means that the wind can be incredibly fluky. It can make racing exceptionally difficult. Yet, crucially, I felt I'd done my preparation as well as, if not better than, most, in terms of time I'd spent getting used to the conditions. Paul Goodison, who was to go on and win a gold in Beijing, was my training partner. He grew up sailing on the lakes in the north of England, where winds can be similar, so it was excellent having him there.

In that final race, I started attacking Robert in the pre-start, manoeuvring to try and force him away from the other boats to the unfavoured side of the course. You can do that, within the rules. You can't just go and ram other sailors off the course. But you can shepherd them and use your right-of-way position to block them, and get bad wind off the sails. If you can put your bad wind directly in front of the other guy it slows him down a huge amount. I started doing that.

My strategy was nearly ruined when the race was postponed halfway through the start – we had to wait about half an hour before the wind settled down again and the race was restarted. Obviously, by then, he knew what I was endeavouring to do. Now he was a bit wiser. He was just sailing round and round the committee boat to keep free from getting caught out. Eventually he split and ran for the middle of the start line. I chased him down there. With about five seconds to go before the start, I got into a leeward position which is a right-of-way position, got underneath and luffed him. He bore away and we just had contact. I protested and he did two penalty turns which put him behind the fleet. I stopped and waited for him, bearing in mind what John had said about ensuring that I put him as far down the fleet as possible. I was directly on his wind already, trying to slow him down. He just put in tack after tack after tack. There must have been fifty tacks up that first upwind leg. As I came through one tack and threw my body out of the boat I almost missed the hiking strap and was literally hanging on by my big toe; I never forget that and how close I came to disaster. He was screaming at me in Portuguese, so frustrated was he at what was happening. Two on-water jury boats were watching us like hawks to make sure no one broke the rules.

It turned into the furious battle it had always promised to become. We were both on top of our game. It was like a boxing match, with two heavyweights eyeball to eyeball. At such times, there's nothing genteel about international competitive sailing.

He was yelling things at me. I'm not sure what he said, but it wasn't very polite. It's a stressful sport. So much goes into it. There are so many thought processes because there are so many variables. It's mentally draining and can be hugely frustrating; that's why some people boil over. It was on a knife-edge. Ferociously intense. But that's what's amazing about competing at the highest level, it's like a drug which drives you on. Every manoeuvre he made, I covered it. He was trying to catch me out, and break free. By this time, we were a long way last. But I still felt I needed more. I set up a trap whereby I kept him to the outside of me, and just wouldn't let him go round the first turning mark. He was really frustrated, as you would be.

Robert turned and gybed his boat straight in front of me and we collided. In the process, he eluded me, and was gone. But I believed he was in the wrong and was quite confident about that. I would protest. He should be disqualified. But I couldn't be absolutely certain he'd receive a guilty verdict once the evidence was reviewed back on shore. More pertinent, for the moment, was the fact that Robert was attempting to regain lost ground. He was capable of it, too.

But would his efforts be enough? I was chasing him, trying to catch him up, and get in front of him. It is testament to his talent that he did an amazing job in those conditions to catch up with the backmarkers.

One more lap to go. I was watching his every move. My mind was working overtime on adrenalin trying to calculate the points, at the same time as trying to work out how to overtake Robert. I was still just behind him. But, remember, he had to catch up to twenty-first place out of the forty boats. I thought there was no way he could do that.

Suddenly we were on the second-to-last leg. I could see this large patch of dark water coming towards us from the other side of the harbour, which was basically signifying a massive wind-shift. Robert had picked that up and gone the opposite way to the whole of the rest of the fleet. He had got this wind and was coming to the next mark at twice the speed of any other boat moving in a straight line. I was powerless to intervene. I thought: 'I don't believe this. He's going to do it.' He went round the final mark in twenty-second place. He just needed to overtake one more boat.

That boat was sailed by a guy from Singapore, Stanley Tan. I sailed down behind them, and I was saying to myself 'Come on, go, Stanley.' In truth, I fully expected Robert to make it, but somehow he just couldn't get past him. Stanley held him off. Robert was one place outside what he needed to win gold. But had I done enough? I'd been lifted out of the water by all my teammates. That was a great feeling. I felt like I'd won, but I wasn't sure. I couldn't celebrate yet. There was also a protest hearing looming.

That was incredibly tense. I'd 'protested' him for the incident that had happened at the windward mark. He'd put in a two-part protest against me – one relating specifically to that windward mark incident, the other saying my tactics weren't fair. As it transpired, he'd made a mistake somehow and had put the protest in out of the allotted time.

The panel of five judges rejected the first part because it was submitted too late. However, they heard his argument regarding the second part, under Rule 2 which relates to 'recognized principles of sportsmanship and fair play' and found that I'd sailed within the rules and they didn't have a problem. Then they heard my protest, and watched a lot of video evidence, and clearly found in my favour.

It was all a huge relief. Protest hearings are notoriously fickle and you can never be certain of the jury's final decision. But this was a complete vindication of my tactics that day. The general reaction was that it had been an amazing race and a real thrill to watch. Not everyone saw it that way, however. Certainly not in Brazil, where feelings had, apparently, been inflamed by my triumph. It was to provoke death threats from supporters of Robert Scheidt and the burning of effigies in his home city, São Paulo. It would even bring condemnation of my tactics by one of Britain's great sporting knights. Sir Roger Bannister was amongst a few observers who commented that it was ridiculous that you could win an Olympic gold medal in the manner I had. His words did leave a bad taste at the time, but it was not something I dwelt on. It's like making judgements about Formula 1 tactics, without understanding the nuances of motor-sport. Only observers who didn't know sailing well enough thought it was wrong. If they'd bothered to do some research about the rules and had scrutinised the race, maybe then they could comment. In Sydney, everything I did was completely within the rules. It was just that it had never really happened on that scale, and at that level, before.

My prime concern was that I'd turned the tables and transformed the silver I'd won in Atlanta as a teenager, four years previously, into gold. It would be the first of three I would win in consecutive Olympics.

After the protest hearings, my parents, Roddy and Sue, were waiting for me. It was a really special moment. They'd been through everything with me, from the day I'd started out in my beginner's dinghy on the creek where we lived in Cornwall. They were waiting outside the venue. By this time it was eight, nine o'clock at night, and it was getting dark. I walked out of a really quiet dinghy park to be confronted by camera flashes and TV lights. Even when he hasn't been there to watch me, my father generally knows how I've done before I give him a call. He's a great sounding board; it's always been good to have him to talk things through with.

I thought back to 1993, when I was 16, and had been invited to the BBC Sports Personality of the Year award. Dad went with me. Loads of fans were milling around when we got out of the taxi outside the Westminster Conference Centre. All these photographers came running towards me. I thought 'Oh, my God. What's happening?' Then someone shouted out: 'Oh, don't worry. It's nobody.' My dad laughed and told me not to worry about it. But it taught me very early on, that the important thing was not about trying to be somebody, it was about getting results and trying to be the best I could be in my sport. Seven years on, I had won a gold medal, the pinnacle of sport, but I was far happier to see my parents than I was the cameras.

They say that Captain Arthur Phillip, commander of the First Fleet of eleven ships, observed on first sighting Sydney in January 1788: 'We got into Port Jackson early in the afternoon, and had the satisfaction of finding the finest harbour in the world.'

That's how I regarded those waters, too, on that pivotal day for me just over a couple of hundred years later. I had won the gold I craved, and, with it, retribution for the events four years earlier.

Chapter 2

That Sinking Feeling

The world over, from the dusty streets of São Paulo to the backyards and rough areas of waste ground of Sunderland, you'll find youngsters kicking a football around. That's undoubtedly the case today, even in health and safety conscious Britain! Kids will always find a way. That's when they start to dream of emulating the great players they watch live or on TV. Never mind the professional coaching that comes their way if they demonstrate themselves talented enough to become professional sportsmen. It's in those early years that they first hone their basic ball control and what's makes them so good at the game.

I had my own backyard – or perhaps backwater is a more appropriate word for the creek in Cornwall – where I first learnt to love sailing. It became my own little haven in which I learnt the basics of a sport which would propel me to three Olympic golds and one silver medal.

I was approaching 8 when our family moved down from Cheshire into the former fisherman's cottage on the edge of Restronguet Creek, near Falmouth. If you had to design a safe water playground for a child, it couldn't have been more perfect.

9

It had many inlets, like gnarled fingers of water, which you could go out exploring to your heart's content. For me, it evoked Swallows and Amazons, Arthur Ransome's series of novels which depicted a world of childhood fantasy, mostly set on water. But this stretch had an even greater significance for me. This idyllic new world soon introduced me to the sport that I love. For that I will always be grateful.

Our creek was no more than three kilometres long, protected from the main inlet to the sea, the Fal Estuary, or the Carrick Roads as it is known, by the peninsula a hundred metres opposite, Restronguet Point. The latter has always been an exclusive place to live, the equivalent of the fashionable Rock in the north of the county. Our side of the creek was rather more modest. We had just a few neighbours and it wasn't readily accessible by road. You had to drive along a couple of hundred metres of beach to reach our cottage, and then up a track. Not everyone's choice of location. But for a young child it added to the magic of the place.

Restronguet Creek is like an inland tidal lake, into which flow waters from the Carnon and the Kennal rivers. It was once an important industrial waterway, a thoroughfare for ships bringing pit props from Norway and Wales for the tin mines inland. They also carried coal, lime and copper ore, which had been brought down the Carnon Valley by the Redruth and Chasewater railway. Today the creek is renowned worldwide for its beauty and its wildlife. For me, back in the mid-eighties onwards, being around boats and being able to mess about on the water all the time was my idea of heaven.

My sailing experience all began in an old wooden beginner's dinghy, an Optimist, which will be familiar to youngsters the world over. It was – I can assure anyone who immediately makes the assumption that my sailing background was somehow privileged – nothing grand.

My parents had bought the old second-hand boat from friends of theirs as a Christmas present for me. I woke up to find this Optimist in front of me. It was a shock as I had never seen a boat this small before but I soon realised it was only designed for kids up the age of 15 and was only supposed to be sailed single-handed.

Designed in 1947, Optimists were originally intended to be the largest possible sailboat that youngsters could build themselves, using two 4ft × 8ft sheets of plywood. Although it has a flat bow, the boat has remarkably good handling characteristics. Mine was numbered 185, so it would have been one of the first ever of its type. It had a wooden mast and a red and yellow sail, and cost no more than £100. Being constructed of wood, it was much heavier than its fibreglass equivalent. It had rubber bumper rings round the side, so that if you crashed into anything you couldn't do too much damage. This proved to be very fortunate. The only problem with the boat's weight was that when I had to push it up the beach, I needed help.

I wasted no time in getting my present on the water that Christmas morning. We took the Optimist, or *Opalong* as the boat was called, down to the beach, and launched it. There was a really nice pub called the Pandora about 400 metres in the opposite direction from our cottage, on the creek. It was the social hub for my parents and their friends. My dad just said casually: 'Off you go. We'll walk up to the pub and see you there for lunch in fifteen minutes.' I'd never sailed on my own before. I just had my duffel coat and wellies on. I asked my dad: 'What happens if I turn the boat over?' He replied: 'Oh, I think you've got to stand on the centre-board to get it back. You'll be all right. See you at the pub.'

And off I set. And, really, that's where it all began; a pastime which was to develop swiftly into an obsession. Initially, it was a voyage of self-discovery, but in its own way, that contributed to the creation of the sailor I am today. Out at sea, the wind's straight all the time and makes sailing a lot easier. In a creek, however, the wind fluctuates and moves direction frequently because of the topography of the land around it. That gives you a real natural feel for the effect the wind has on sailing. It means you very quickly learn to adapt to different wind conditions.

When I came home from my primary school there weren't many other young children living near me to play with, so, quite often, I'd just hoist the sail and set off; just as my contemporaries throughout the world would take a ball out to play. It was so much fun for me to go out sailing right there on my doorstep. It was my release.

That first outing went fine. It was not always so. Once, about a year after I was given my Optimist, I was sailing around on my own, I went to tack, and my foot became tangled in the toe strap (the webbing under which you hook your feet when sitting out) and the mainsheet (the rope attached to the boom which is used to trim the mainsail). I couldn't move across the boat, and it capsized on top of me, with my foot still trapped. It was quite scary. There was a little air pocket underneath the upturned boat and I was there for several minutes. Fortunately, an older boy in his boat arrived, saw that I was in trouble, jumped on my boat and brought it upright. His name was Paul Pullen, and he and his brother, Matt, would become really good friends of mine. I'd have probably been fine, but it taught me a lesson. And, even today, over twenty years on, I'm still learning them.

All this time my father, Roddy, had taken more than a normal paternal interest. He had been a big-boat sailor, who had been skipper of *Second Life* in the first Whitbread Round the World race (now known as the Volvo Ocean Race) of 1973–4. Today there are several such ocean challenges open to sailors. Not then. This was something new entirely, and great excitement amongst sailors accompanied the announcement that Whitbread, the brewing company, and the British Royal Naval Sailing Association were collaborating to sponsor the first crewed, global yacht race. The original course was designed to follow the route of the square riggers, which had carried cargo around the world during the nineteenth century.

Some of the skippers were, inevitably, highly experienced men of the sea, and none more so than Chay Blyth, a British Army sergeant who, in 1966, had rowed the Atlantic with Captain John Ridgway in a six-metre dory. Also, two years before that first Whitbread, he had become the first person to sail non-stop westwards around the world aboard the twenty-one-metre ketch *British Steel*. In that first Whitbread he skippered *Great Britain II*, funded by Bahamian philanthropist 'Union' Jack Hayward.

But many were keen amateurs, with only limited experience of offshore sailing. My father was one of those, and he had formed a syndicate with his brother-in-law Ian Butterworth and found twelve paying passengers to take their chartered Ocean 71 around the course. Everyone paid £3,000, and the entire project cost £40,000.

My sailing connections with the race don't end there. My godfather, Les Williams, a former naval yachtsman, who with Robin Knox-Johnston had won the 1970 Round Britain Race, was skipper of the UK's *Burton Cutter*, which at twenty-four metres was the biggest yacht in the fleet. Les also had a young Kiwi in his crew called Peter Blake who would go on to become one of the most successful and respected sailors of all time.

My mother had originally planned to take part too, as cook on *Second Life* – until fate intervened. My parents had always thought they couldn't have children, but a month before the race started, she found herself pregnant for the first time. While my father was at sea, she gave birth to my sister, Fleur. In hindsight, perhaps it was a good thing that she didn't make it. It would have been an arduous ordeal.

But a total of seventeen yachts and 167 crew did start that first race of 27,500 nautical miles, setting out from Portsmouth on 8 September 1973. Around 3,000 spectator boats were there at the start. Dad and his crew not only finished, but were seventh overall, which was a magnificent achievement.

Three years after Fleur was born, I made my entrance on 5 February 1977. I was born in Macclesfield, in the area south of Manchester from which both my parents hailed. My father was from near Knutsford and my mother from Wilmslow. My father had just taken charge of his family's business. Originally, it had been a medium-sized company, manufacturing wire fences. When my dad became involved, they diversified and started making all kinds of wooden products: kitchen tabletops, spade handles, right down to those old wooden rulers you used to get in stationers. He had been involved in the business earlier but went off and concentrated on sailing for around five years, before returning to take over the business from his father. My grandmother, grandfather, uncle and aunt on his side also had a share in the company.

My parents had met at school, and got married when my mum was 19. My dad was two years older. They are not too far off celebrating their golden wedding. They have always got on really well and my sister and I were very fortunate to have parents who enjoyed each other's company and were really committed to having a happy family life.

My grandfather on my father's side once started tracing the family tree. He went as far back as finding out that our ancestors were Scottish, and were all hung for stealing sheep on the south side of the border. He stopped there. He probably got a bit disillusioned by that stage. I saw a lot of him and my grandmother at the family business as I used to hang around the yard some Saturdays.

On my mother's side, my grandfather was a Spitfire pilot in the Second World War. He was based at RAF Ringwood, south of Manchester. I used to love sitting with him, and listening to stories about his sorties. He achieved a notoriety in the war. There was an order that attacks should not include religious sites, such as churches or cathedrals. On one mission, his squadron was attacking Cologne, and he managed to damage the city's cathedral, getting himself into a huge amount of trouble in the process. My great-grandfather on my mother's side made a name for himself as an inventor.

My elder sister Fleur has two young children, Tansy and Oscar. They are lovely children and I really enjoy spending time with them. They are just starting to get into sailing which is great and has already led to a few amusing situations. Fleur is married to a Dutchman, Jerome Pels, who is the Secretary General of the International Sailing Federation. So, as you can imagine, we have a few heated conversations about the world of sailing around the dinner table.

As a young child, the Cheshire countryside was my playground. We lived in a nice house adjoining a working farm. A friend and I would often run over to the farm and play in the hay bales. We would always be annoying the farmer by constantly knocking over his neatly stacked bales. And worse. One day, we got into a tractor and somehow managed to start it, including the large crop-cutting blades. Fortunately it didn't move off, but we couldn't work out how to stop it. I had to slink back home and come clean to my mother who demanded that I should find the farmer immediately, and apologise.

I have wonderful memories of that time, although as the 'baby' of the family I tended to suffer most when I was left with my sister and our cousin – my mother's brother's daughter – called Sorell, who was four or five years older than me. She had a highly vivid imagination and, when she came round to play, got us doing some weird and wacky things. Once my parents and aunt and uncle were sitting in the dining room, having a drink, when polythene bags came floating down past the window. It was suspiciously quiet upstairs, so my mum investigated and found me – I was about 2 at the time – perched on the windowsill with my sister and cousin about to push me out of the window with a polythene bag under each arm. They thought the bags would act like parachutes! Fortunately my mum got hold of me before I took my first flying lesson.

Overall, though, I can honestly say they were really happy times. I was very fortunate. You read of some sports personalities who, in part, achieve what they do almost as a consequence of troubled childhoods. For boxers, the ring has often been a means of escaping the poverty and deprivation of broken homes. It was never like that for me. My parents were always supportive of my sister and me. They were fine role models; good people. The only problems I ever encountered, as I will explain later, were at school. From the age of 3, I attended a good independent preschool called Terra Nova, with small classes, about five miles away. I never took to it that well, but made lots of friends there.

It did not take long for my parents to introduce me to sailing. I was 3 or 4 when my parents bought a small cruising boat which was kept at Holyhead, a two- or three-hour drive away. They'd take my sister, Fleur, and I with them and we went on trips across the Irish Sea or around Conway. That was my intro-duction to sailing. Dad says that I was immediately fascinated by water. I don't remember much about it, though it always seemed pretty rough on the Irish Sea.

By the time I was 6 or 7, my father had bought a classic yawl, which is a two-masted craft, from a member of the Guinness family. It was a McGruer, a beautiful boat, but was in a really bad state of repair when he got it. We took her down the Manchester Ship Canal to a boatyard at Northwich where he spent two years rebuilding her. He worked on the project every weekend. The skills required came easily to him. The business he was involved in meant he had a woodworking background. He did an amazing job; restoring the yawl as it had been in its heyday. It was quite beautiful when they finished it.

Dad retired quite young, in his late 40s. I guess he was entitled to do so, because he had worked seriously hard throughout his life. We didn't see him that much during the week. He'd left in the morning by the time we'd got up. He wouldn't get home until around eight o'clock most of the time and, by then, my sister and I were in bed. That's why it was great when he had time for us, and that was mainly at weekends, although he also worked most Saturdays, too.

We had moved from Cheshire to Cornwall when I was 7. Dad had decided to sell the family business. That industry was dying a slow death because of the emergence of plastics and he decided to get out of it. We had some family friends who lived down in the West Country and we'd spent a few summers on holiday there. They'd seen a cottage for sale and had fallen in love with it. For my parents, it was the ideal setting. In addition, Fleur and I were both young enough that we could switch schools without too much disruption to our education. So, my parents went for it. I'm exceptionally glad they did. At the time, I was thrilled by the prospect of moving to live by the sea.

I was always fascinated by the water and the way boats moved in it. I didn't have to be out sailing. We also had a rowing boat, and I just enjoyed going out and sitting in the middle of the creek and watching the world go by. It was an environment I loved. I made friends who lived around the Fal Estuary, and there was one particular boy who lived on the other side of the creek. We both had dinghies. Sometimes we'd meet in the middle. Or I'd sail across to his house, or he'd come to mine. Those were really happy times.

Would I have had the career I did, and been as successful as I was, if we hadn't moved to Cornwall? Who can say. It wasn't as if my parents said 'Oh, Ben's going to be a future Olympic champion. Let's move to Cornwall because that would be good for his sailing.' I was just really lucky that was the way it worked out.

I said earlier that I didn't have a particularly privileged background. Yet, I could do what only a few young boys could: I could sail whenever the fancy took me, or maybe take out a rowing boat or motorboat. That gave me a wonderful sense of freedom. Even if you lost a rudder or something fell off you'd eventually drift into the shoreline.

I have to laugh when I recall those years. When you think how mollycoddled kids are today, with all the concern for children's health and safety, and here I was, at 8 or 9, sailing around on my own in my Optimist; even sometimes in the dark. I suspect that, nowadays, parents would be highly concerned if that was happening. I was quite lucky. My parents placed a lot of trust in me and were quite content to let me go off and sail.

In terms of what I do now, being on the water from a very early age gave me confidence. Also there was the fact that people we met on family trips would talk about sailing, and even maybe racing. Even at that age, 7 or 8, I was intrigued. I guess it gets ingrained in you a bit and I enjoyed hearing the stories of local fishermen and racing sailors, guys like Timmy Bailey. It was something I got to love more and more as I got older.

Meanwhile my dad was luxuriating in his idea of paradise. He could now sail the yawl he had so lovingly restored around the Cornwall coast, and from so close to home, too. We'd do many short trips, like sailing from Falmouth round to Fowey. It was an enjoyable social scene, and my parents made many friends who had boats. We also had a lot of family holidays. One time, to my great excitement, we sailed over to the Brittany coast for around three weeks.

We had some pretty hairy moments; particularly the first night, trying to get into the harbour. Dad was a pretty good navigator, but a heavy fog had descended. These, remember, were the days before GPS navigation. There were strong tides and it was very quiet. Too quiet. Suddenly the fog lifted and, from nowhere, a lighthouse just loomed up before us, and we were confronted by some nasty-looking rocks. Miraculously, Dad somehow managed to negotiate a tiny gap into a lagoon in front of the lighthouse. My mum, who was a good sailor and normally enjoyed it all, just about freaked out. We were still in a precarious position. After a while, I said to my dad: 'How are we going to get out of here?' 'Well,' he replied patiently, 'I think we'll just turn around and go back the way we came in.' It probably wasn't all that dangerous a situation but at that age I remember being in awe of how calm my dad was in such a precarious position.

A year or so later, however, we were not so fortunate. Much nearer home we were shipwrecked. It was a traumatic episode for everyone but especially my father as he had to watch his pride and joy wrecked before his eyes. Yet, the incident indirectly kick-started my sailing career.

One of our outings was to sail from our home, round past Falmouth and down to the Helford River which is a really beautiful spot. It's about twenty miles, a three- or four-hour sail. Normally, we'd set off in the morning, stop and have lunch there and return in the afternoon. One Easter, we started out with myself, my sister, my parents and a friend of theirs, Brian Bellingham, who was a naval helicopter pilot and also a very good sailor, plus a school friend of mine.

Conditions were fine, and we reached the Helford River. It's quite narrow, only about half a mile across at the entrance. My dad went to start the engine, but there was no response. He realised that he couldn't steer, either. We'd run over a lobster pot. Because it was a classic yacht the keel was much longer than normal. The rudder was an extension of the keel and the propeller was located between the two. The lobster pot had wrapped itself around the propeller.

We couldn't use the engine *or* the rudder, so we couldn't steer, *and* we still had all the sails up. We couldn't get them down quickly enough. I could see these rocks approaching, and I remember my dad and Brian desperately trying to trim sails in an attempt to turn the boat. I was trying to help too, as best as you can at 8 or 9, by trying to wind in one of the sails. We didn't make it and the boat smashed into the rocks and became caught in a gully. I recall being amazed at how calm my father was in the situation.

Having got my sister, myself, my friend and my mum off the boat, on to the rocks and on to a pathway to safety, Dad and Brian got the sails down and then tried really hard to clear the propeller and get it off the rocks. If he'd been lucky it would have bounced off them. But these were jagged rocks. A fibreglass boat would have been smashed to pieces. This wooden craft was strong, and remained in one piece, but it was fatally damaged.

We set off some flares and called a lifeboat, but that took about an hour and a half to come round from Falmouth. They dragged the boat off the rocks, and tried to get pumps on to it in time but the boat went straight to the bottom. It was really a terrible sight. Dad had put so much effort into it. He'd spent two years solidly restoring it, although boats like that you never stop working on. They take a lot of maintenance.

They were able to salvage the yawl a couple of weeks later, but the problem was that it had been so badly damaged. You have a stem which is basically the spine of the boat to which all the ribs are joined. That was broken. It effectively means the whole boat has to be rebuilt. He just didn't have the will for it.

Dad has owned a number of boats since then. Soon after, he bought a racing boat, a Lightwave 395, a 40ft cruiser-racer, and did a double-handed Round Britain Race with a good friend, Peter Visick. It was his way of getting over that experience, and around ten years ago, he bought a Folk Boat, a very small classic boat designed to sleep two or three people. I had a few adventures on her myself, cruising around, running into rocks and all sorts.

I took it for a few expeditions with my girlfriend at the time. One Easter, I received very clear instructions about negotiating Gillan Harbour which is just round the coast from Helford River, near where my parents now live and where the boat was moored. A buoy was marking a rock. I had clear instructions about which side of the buoy to go to clear the rock. Which we did – and still managed to run aground.

I was down below getting a sail and pretty much headbutted the mast as the boat stopped on the rock. I cursed and ran on deck to give the poor girl on the helm a hard time for not paying any attention to what I had said. I then grabbed the helm and proceeded to do exactly the same thing again, much to my girlfriend's amusement and my embarrassment as we had now become stuck on the rock. A local boatman had to come out and tow us off the rock and for some reason he had pretty good chuckle about it.

But to return to the sinking of my father's yawl, it was a bit of a news story in Cornwall, with Dad having competed in the Whitbread. We had a phone call from a woman named Jill Slater, who'd read about the sinking. She and her husband, Dr Phil Slater, a GP, who was a major local sailing figure, had started a coaching clinic for youngsters – including their own children, Matthew and Verity, who were a similar age to me – at the nearby sailing club, in Mylor Churchtown. Hearing that I had an Optimist, she invited me to take my boat down there and learn how to sail. I didn't require a second invitation.

Chapter 3

From the Boys in the Barracudas to the Best of British

Within a year, Dr Phil and Jill Slater had gone out and encouraged around forty of us youngsters down to the Restronguet Sailing Club. That was based about half an hour away from my home by boat. It was all organised in a child-friendly fashion. We were split into three groups. The beginners, just learning to sail, were called the Parrots. It was designed to be fun, with follow-the-leader expeditions, and prizes at the end. Maybe there'd be a picnic. Jill, who possessed an ideal manner about her with young children, coached the Parrots.

The Barracudas group was a little bit more serious, and was aimed to get the boys and girls into racing. They were coached by a fellow called Eddie Shelton. He was the father of a good friend of mine, Jamie Shelton. Eddie was a good sailor, who contributed a lot to our sailing education. By trade, he was a marine engineer, and had quite a smart speedboat. One day, he took Jamie and me out on it, and in Falmouth Harbour we were rewarded by the spectacle of two 12m yachts sailing past us. They turned out to be the America's Cup boats, *Victory 83*, and the B boat, owned by the entrepreneur Peter de Savary. At that time, de Savary's British America's Cup team was based out at Port Falmouth. For us Optimist kids, that was an awesome experience.

I thought 'That's great. I'd really love to do that one day.' I was only about 12 at the time. I don't know if it was remarkable prescience or not, but Eddie told me: 'One day, you'll be doing that.' I've never forgotten those words. I laughed off the observation. But he was persistent. He said: 'Yes. You keep going, you'll get there.' That was quite an inspiration, so early on, and quite a poignant moment. It was a prospect that would long fuel my imagination.

The elite at our sailing club were the Aces. Phil Slater was in charge of them. That was deadly serious, all about racing, with the aim of trying to encourage the very best to compete nationally. The Slaters, who still live in Falmouth, did so much for sailing in the area. My early years would be very reliant on Phil's expertise and advice.

I started off with the Parrots, sailing my wooden boat. Then I progressed quickly to the Barracudas. Even in my slow old boat I started beating guys who were in the Aces. In time, Phil told my dad that I was doing really well, but I needed a better boat because mine was too heavy, and in racing, a heavy dinghy is a slow dinghy. The only advantage was that everybody got out of my way, because if I hit another boat it could cause serious damage. And I had plenty of collisions.

Sailing has always brought the competitive instincts out of me, maybe sometimes to excess. Though I enjoyed sports like football and cricket, I had never been particularly brilliant at them. But sailing was something I really enjoyed. Even early on, I sensed I had a flair for it. I was determined to do well in the sport, and it made me super-competitive. I simply hated losing; even as a child. I just refused to be beaten by anyone.

As youngsters learning to sail and race we were lucky it was such a nice club, with so many well-intentioned adults who helped us. In part that was because Phil was such a prominent, high-profile member of the club, and was really trying to do something with the youngsters, ensuring the rest of the club really embraced us. There were always lots of experienced sailors who would answer your questions. And this being Cornwall, they were always pretty laid-back.

My dad would also get involved from time to time. He had never been a dinghy sailor, but he picked up things as we went along. At mealtimes, we'd chat about the racing and sailing. We'd both speak to Phil about what I needed to do better.

It took me a while to get the hang of things. When I started out, still in the old wooden Optimist, I wasn't exactly reckless, but I'd go out in any conditions even though I didn't really know what I was doing. They had a couple of rescue boats down at the club. Every time they saw me coming down, the guy who was in charge of them would apparently observe: 'Oh, no. It's that Ainslie kid again. We'll have to get the rescue boats ready.' I'd just set off with the wind behind me, and I wouldn't know how to get back. I'd reach the other side of the estuary, it'd be blowing hard and I'd get stuck. They had to come out, pick me up and tow me back in. This happened continually for about a month.

Fortunately, there was a really nice guy around called Terry White, whose son had been a very good Optimist sailor before I started. Eventually, he said: 'I'm going to have to show you how to do this. We can't keep launching the boat and coming out after you.' As it turned out, it wouldn't be the last time that I've needed rescuing in my sailing career.

I wasn't a total novice about the technicalities. I understood the basics of that from the big-boat sailing I'd done with my family. Obviously I knew that a boat needs to tack into the wind. But there's some big differences with dinghies. You can turn a dinghy over and capsize it. You can't do that with a yacht. I had to learn all that: how to use your body weight to balance the boat, and to react more with the waves. All that took a little bit of getting used to.

Eventually, a couple of years after I started, my dad bought me a much lighter, fibreglass boat so that I could race effectively. It had been owned by a girl who had won the national championships a couple of years previously. It wasn't brand new, but it was a really good boat, well set up. The transition was immediate. Suddenly I was winning races. Having been in a heavy slow boat, once I got into that, I was off like a rocket.

We trained on Saturday and Sunday mornings, and raced on Sunday afternoons in a club series of fleet races. We had two races which lasted about an hour each. To me it felt like the most competitive racing of any club anywhere. Even by my standards today, some of the racing we did then was fiercer than most of what I've encountered since.

By then I was in the top group, where two other boys stuck out from the crowd: David Lenz and Darren Williams. We three were so into our sailing; we'd read all the books, we knew who all the sailing personalities were, people like the Kiwi Russell Coutts, who has won the America's Cup as a skipper three times, and is, arguably, the world's finest yachtsman. He and his compatriot Chris Dickson – New Zealand produces top sailors like they do the world's best rugby players – were the guys we wanted to emulate.

David, Darren and I would take each other out and be super-aggressive, because that's how we'd heard Dickson and Coutts were. We thought that's the way you needed to be. It got us all used to pushing the opposition really hard.

We travelled to events elsewhere in the country, though logistically, because we were in Cornwall, that was not always easy and there was heavy reliance on parental support. We were necessarily quite insular. We only did four or five events – regattas – a year. So, we made the racing within our own club count. It was really focussed. It meant a lot more to us.

Phil Slater identified the youngsters who were doing well, and tried to encourage them to be even more ambitious and compete in national events. That's how I ended up travelling up to the national championships at Largs, near Glasgow, in 1988. Phil had a word with my dad and recommended that I enter. It was an astute suggestion. It represented a dramatic improvement in such a relatively short time, particularly considering that I had no experience of racing in a big fleet. I was used to competing with no more than ten rivals. Suddenly, here I was amongst 150.

I was helped by the fact that also taking part that year there was a really friendly guy, also from Restronguet, called Nicky Quintrell, who had done well internationally, and been in GB's world championship team. He was very helpful to me, in part because this was his last year at the club as he was 15. I basically followed him and his friend, Jim Gorrod, from Southampton, who was also at the head of the fleet, and followed them round the course. I had no real idea what I was doing. But they did. I finished about thirtieth overall, but won the junior section, the under-12s.

I had so much to take in. But I was really proud of that victory. There was another guy sailing close to me I knew I had to beat to win. It was the first time my competitive instincts at an important event had emerged.

Within three or four years of our Restronguet Sailing Club elite group being set up, we had advanced from having no one really competing internationally to being the top club in the country. It was astonishing progress, and the direct result of us driving each other on. I can't emphasise that enough. We had three or four boats in the top ten. I count myself really lucky to come through in that period. Two of us, David Lenz and myself, made the world championship team, which consisted of the top five young sailors in the country. It was a huge achievement for the club. At a very early stage, it taught me the importance of having good people to train against.

Throughout the year, there were regular training camps at Weymouth or Rutland Water in Leicestershire. There was no let-up. Even in winter, on three weekends, we had to drive up to Rutland from Cornwall for those camps. One of the parents would drive us all, with our boats on the trailer behind. It involved an eight-hour drive each way, between which we'd go sailing in bitterly cold conditions. We'd usually get back home at two on the Monday morning.

There were moments of light relief. I recall the many events held down in Cornwall during the summer. Through Falmouth Week, each day one of the villages in the area would hold its regatta. It'd be the Falmouth Regatta, the St Mawes Regatta or the Restronguet Regatta. We'd go round and race in our Optimists during the week. One of the traditional highlights – and which still goes on today – was racing between the famous, gaff-rigged working boats, particularly characteristic of Falmouth.

There are very rich oyster beds down there. Rather than have engine-powered fishing boats raking up the beds and depleting the oyster stocks, all the fishing boats had to be sail-powered. Compared with small Optimists, these craft were massive, and you'd find members of the local rugby team helping out with the crewing.

We'd be sailing our Optimists, and we'd have right of way over the working boats. So, you'd get a 10-year-old 'Oppy kid', as we were called, yelling at them to give way. The crew's stock answer tended to be 'Bugger off'. We loved the banter. That was always good fun.

In so many ways during this period, life could not have been better, although I can't say things were going quite so well off the water – and particularly at school where I tended to spend most of my time thinking about sailing and how I was going to make my boat go faster.

My schooldays were not an easy time for me. I suffered and still do suffer from a skin photosensitivity. It causes my skin to blister and come out in a rash. As we all know, children can be pretty insensitive to that sort of thing. When I was young the rash was often on my face which prompted a lot of teasing from the other kids and this was something I wasn't able to shake off until my mid teens when I finally left school in Cornwall. It's easy to shrug it off now but writing this book and thinking back to that period, it does make me wince slightly.

When we first made our home in Cornwall, I went to Treliske School. It was the preschool for the adjacent, private Truro School. At 11, I took the entrance exams to Truro School, and passed those. Now I look at things differently and wish I'd been as focussed on my studies as I was on my sailing. Then, I was just a kid and not really interested. I got through school because I had to. I spent a lot of time staring out of the window, thinking about boats and sailing. I feel an element of guilt that I didn't try hard enough at school, especially as it was a serious expense for my parents to pay for the education in the first place.

It is a shame that I wasn't really more motivated by school. If there was a theme that ran through my reports it was that I tried hard but needed to pay more attention. Somehow, I got through. I was always very good at listening to what the teachers were saying while actually thinking about something else. There was a Biology teacher, Dr Ganey, who scared the living daylights out of us. He'd always try and catch me out. '*Ainslie*, what did I just say?' he'd ask me. I had a very good knack of being able to respond correctly, and tell him, without actually paying any attention whatsoever. It used to frustrate the hell out of him. Unfortunately, it didn't mean I remembered any of it when it came to exam time.

The bullying began at the end of junior school. Children tend to isolate anyone who's different, even very slightly. I have to say it was pretty hard to deal with and I probably didn't handle it in the best possible way as I am naturally quite a shy person. Unfortunately it began at my first school and continued through to the main school as I stuck with the same pupils over a seven-year period and they never really gave me a break.

Like all things the teasing came and went, but I guess it did have a profound effect on how I developed. It made me ferociously determined to be good at something to prove to myself that I could be a success and that there was more to life than school and being picked on. Sadly, it also meant that I found it hard to trust people, was very defensive and found it very difficult to open up to people emotionally.

Despite all this, I somehow managed to scrape my way

through my exams. I took GCSEs in subjects including Maths, English, History, Geography. I also got an A in Craft, Design and Technology – completely to the dismay of my teacher Dennis Kean who was another irritated by my lack of attention. He had actually phoned my dad at home at one stage, and said 'I've got real problems with Ben. I don't think he should carry on in this subject because he's not going to pass.' Dad and I had quite an amusing conversation. 'Er, what did you say?' I asked Dad. He replied: 'I told him that it was his job, as your teacher, to make sure that you do pass!' It was typical of my dad and I loved him for that. In the end it was quite ironic that I ended up getting an A grade in Design and Technology. Every now and then I would go down to breakfast and he'd ask me what I had on at school and suggest that he really needed a hand to take the boat for a sail. Those were wonderful trips where he and I would just disappear for a few days and would decide where to go depending on the wind direction.

As for girls, I was definitely a slow starter. When I was 12 or 13, the school went from being all boys to co-ed, which got everyone excited but I wasn't really one of the gang. Because of my shyness I always found it hard to talk to the girls and be natural, and I also have this incredible ability to put my foot in it and say completely the wrong thing. Fortunately I am much better with people these days, but I still manage to talk myself into some very tricky situations.

Thankfully, I had my sailing to lift my spirits away from school. It made me so determined to do well. To have a sport like that, which I was really good at, was my way of giving myself confidence, proving to myself that I could do something. On the water, following that triumph up at Largs in 1988, I was making great progress.

I had been so buoyed by that, it was no longer a case of receiving encouragement from my parents. They actually had to try and rein me in. I just wanted to do everything I could and enter every event. Realistically that wasn't going to happen, because of the cost. I did the same programme as the other guys at the club. But at the end of that year, I also trained over the winter before competing for the first time in the national trials: a qualification regatta for the world championship team, held at Weymouth.

The top five go through and I finished third. I was still only 12, which was very young to qualify for the world team. Nobody had anticipated that. It certainly created more than a few ripples within the fleet. In the Optimist class back then there were a lot of established families in the sport with youngsters who were always expected to excel. And yet David Lenz and myself had emerged from this little-known club down in Cornwall to finish in the top five. David's achievement was not quite so surprising; he was a year older than me, and a much more experienced sailor. But certainly it took many aback that I had qualified.

The world championships were held in Yokohama, Japan. I was completely out of my depth. Probably too young as well. At 12, I was blown away by everything. Including the winds! The problem was that we thought there would be light winds. That would have suited me because of my slight build. But a typhoon came over and it blew like crazy. I finished around eightieth, and was miles off the pace. It wasn't the greatest of starts to my international career.

The worst aspect was that I didn't even know *why* I hadn't done well. I had believed from an early age that I was quite talented. It was only later that I realised young people develop at different stages. It was not until I got to around 14 or 15 that it became clear to me that it was no good only relying on coaches to tell me which way to go and how to set up the boat. I realised that I'd have to work it all out for myself. Then I started developing very quickly. Since then, so much of my career has been about self-discovery.

Yet if there was one man who had a great influence over my career and those around me during those formative years it was Jim Saltonstall, a remarkable character. I was a member of the Optimist world championship team from 1989 for four years running, and that involved special coaching from Jim. In fact, he had an impact on my career until 1996. He's a legend in his field. He taught us how to race, the basic theory of yacht racing. But more than that, Jim had a passion for the sport which was infectious. He passed his enthusiasm on to us. Gave us the dream.

He was the guy who said to us: 'You can be Olympic champions, you can do the America's Cup, if you train hard and work hard and do things right.' Many British Olympic sailors were coached and mentored by him as youngsters. Apart from myself, their names have included Iain Percy, Andrew Simpson, Sarah Ayton, Chris Draper, Nick Dempsey, Nick Rogers and Joe Glanfield, who all secured youth world championship medals. A great man. In more recent years, Jim has been a global coach, passing on his expertise and helping undeveloped countries at youth world championships.

As I have said already, you only race Optimists until you are 15. In my last year in that class, 1992, I won the UK Optimist national championships. Then I moved into the Laser Radial class, which is similar to the Laser, but has a slightly smaller sail. It's a perfect transition boat for someone light coming out of an Optimist.

That year, 1993, I won the Laser Radial world championships in New Zealand and the Laser Radial European championships. My parents had encouraged me all the way. I felt I had given something back to them by winning the national champion-ships. But to go straight from that to winning the world championships in New Zealand in February was more than they, or I, could have foreseen. It gave me a massive boost in confidence.

It impressed even my tormentors at school. To my relief, by the time I reached 14, the bullying had receded, and things had improved. Maybe at that age, youngsters mature a bit. But significantly once they realised I was a world champion, all of a sudden I started receiving a lot more respect.

I'd been away sailing virtually every weekend. Initially, my school mates either weren't aware, or weren't interested in what I was doing. After that world championships triumph, the attitude towards me miraculously changed; it's amazing how shallow people can be. They suddenly started saying: 'Oh, God, you're a world champion. We didn't realise you were any good at it.' Frankly, I wasn't bothered what they thought. But by the end of my schooling, life became much more fun and bearable. I guess kids grow out of these things. I got on a lot better with everyone.

When I was 15, we moved to Hampshire to be closer to my sister Fleur, who had gone to City University. Also I was doing more sailing around the Southampton area. I left Truro School and started attending Peter Symonds College in Winchester. It had originally been a grammar school but was now a sixth-form college. Its alumni include several well-known entertainment personalities, including comedian Jack Dee. But in particular, there was a boy who became a great friend, Iain Percy.

I had first come across Iain when I started racing Optimists. I used to get quite a bit of grief from the older kids because I was new to the class and had bucked the trend. He was already one of the very established Optimist sailors. His sister Katrina, before him, had been a good Optimist sailor too.

Iain left the Optimist class early, and went off and did some other sailing. But I still saw him every now and again. When I went to Peter Symonds College, Iain was in the year above me there. By that time, we had both moved into the Lasers, so we'd be competing against each other, fighting for that youth world championship place. Initially, that troubled me. I was concerned that I would be perceived as a threat to him on the water. I had moved on to Iain's 'turf'. He'd been to school in Southampton, and had friends at Peter Symonds College. He was the cool man in college, if you like, and I was the outsider. I remember thinking: 'This could be really hard. He could make my life really difficult here.'

He was almost completely the opposite. He really took me under his wing. We've been best mates ever since. He introduced me to all his friends, his social scene, and looked after me. We had a great time training together and we got on really well. I've always been very grateful for that.

On the water, I had maintained my progress. In 1994, I went to the youth national championships which served as trials for the youth world championships. I won – narrowly beating Iain in the process – but the victory was short-lived. Jim Saltonstall was the selection panel for the youth team. The choice was between Iain and me. In one race, Iain was having a bad time of it while I was racing for first with another competitor. I pulled off what I accept was a bizarre move on this guy. Even now I'm not sure how I did it, but I won the race.

Jim was watching all this and for some reason decided to protest me! He wanted me disqualified because of that manoeuvre. I didn't understand his reasoning and so felt it was unfair. I even nursed the thought that he wanted Iain to win those trials and go to the youth world championships, rather than me. I was really annoyed. In the event, the jury threw his protest out. But even then, I still felt nervous that somehow I wouldn't be selected. In fact I was, but it took me some time to get over that and trust Jim again. Fortunately, we developed a really good relationship after that.

I had to settle for a silver in the ISAF youth world championships in 1994. It was all part of a steep learning curve. I had a real battle with a Kiwi lad who's still a great friend, Dan Slater. Dan won, although we were tied on points. However, he won because of a better discard. Effectively, I was denied the gold by one place in one race. Whilst I was shattered by missing out by such a narrow margin it taught me the importance of always striving for your best placing, even if you've no chance of winning a race.

I was learning fast. I had to, because I was never good at dealing with failure. It desperately mattered that I won. I put so much pressure on myself, probably too much. To most people's amusement I could really lose it if I was sailing badly or made a stupid mistake. It was only because I cared so much, but it didn't help my sailing and the sooner I learnt that, and focussed on the racing instead, the better my performances became. Though I've matured, obviously, that desire has never really changed.

The following year, 1995, I won gold at the ISAF youth world championships in the Laser class. Indeed, the event in Bermuda was a particularly good one for British interests. I won in my class and good friends of mine from Lymington, Nick

Rogers and Pom Green, won in the double-handed class. Britain also won the overall team trophy. That was a really good way to finish off my time in the youth squad, and with Jim, particularly as that year the whole team won the British Young Sailor of the Year award.

I also competed in my first senior Laser world championships in 1994 and 1995. The former was held in Japan. I finished forty-second. It was windy and I struggled as I had not fully developed and was too light. The following year, in Tenerife, the conditions were also very windy. I was twenty-first, so I was improving, but I was still not big enough, or strong enough. Not compared with a certain Robert Scheidt, who won his first world championships in Tenerife and set a new benchmark as the man to beat.

Fortuitously, just as I had moved into the Lasers they announced that it would be the new Olympic class for men. It meant that we were training not just for the youth worlds but also against the top senior guys going for the Olympics. That gave me a shot at the Olympic trials at Weymouth that summer, ahead of the Atlanta Games. It turned out to be a remarkable year.

Chapter 4

My Early Promise Goes on Trial

Out of the blue, a guy called Mark Littlejohn, who had been a leading Laser sailor for the last ten years and had reached his early 30s, phoned up. He was looking for someone as a training partner in his bid to win a place in the GB squad for the 1996 Games. He'd seen me racing, and was impressed by my attitude. Mark was massively motivated. As far as I recall, he'd split up with his wife and given up his job in the pursuit of glory. For me, it was an awesome opportunity to learn from one of the top Laser sailors in the country. I agreed without much persuasion and so Mark and I went off and trained all winter down at Weymouth.

It meant calling a halt to my education at Peter Symonds College. I was halfway through my second year when the Laser became an Olympic event. It was basically a decision between full-time training in a bid to qualify for the Olympics – or finishing off my A levels. I couldn't do both. I decided on the former, or at least for the time being. I planned to return to my education afterwards.

Dad was, as ever, a hundred per cent behind me. He has always been so supportive; offering a voice of experience, but almost always backing my decisions. He was keen that I should realise my potential. My mum was always a little more circumspect, and was a bit concerned about me just going off sailing, to the detriment of my education. She'd have preferred it if I'd have passed my A levels first – which, indeed, was also the advice of the RYA (the Royal Yachting Association, British sailing's governing body). But I knew what I wanted to do, and I wouldn't be deflected from that ambition.

My parents have never been pushy types. But they never had a second thought about backing me. They made huge sacrifices before my sponsors came along, and before National Lottery money was available. I feel guilty when I look back and think of what they did to help my career. They weren't particularly wealthy and so it was a big sacrifice for them to help me out financially in my campaign to win a place at the 1996 Olympics. Thankfully, their support made a difference and it was worth it. Dad still helps me out a lot and looks after all my accounts. I think he still gets shocked by how much money I manage to spend.

In my younger days, I was always a worrier and I felt this overwhelming need to get on in life. I was aware I had this talent, and I couldn't let opportunities pass me by. There was this constant concern that they wouldn't arise again. When they presented themselves, I *had* to make the most of them. I really felt I needed to qualify for the Olympics in '96. Once there, I needed to do well. There was never any question of just going for the experience.

The next August, I went out and won the qualifying regatta against all the top guys in the country. They included Mark

Littlejohn and Richard Stenhouse, Chris Gowers, who's now a Laser coach and supported Paul Goodison (known as 'Goody') at Athens and Beijing, Ed Wright, who I am still racing against in the Finn class, Hugh Styles, who was third at the European championships, Gareth Kelly, the national champion, Simon Cole, who had finished in the top three at numerous world championships and two other talented young sailors who would also go on to win gold medals in Beijing: Andrew Simpson (invariably referred to as 'Bart') and Iain Percy.

So, as you can imagine from that line-up, the racing was full on. Very intense. Everyone believed they had a chance. Looking back, they were probably the most hotly contested trials there have been in the UK for many years. There were around fifty Laser sailors taking part, amongst whom possibly eight guys could have won it. And a threat to all the established figures was this callow teenager from Cornwall.

I soon discovered that, as a youngster, and only 18 at that, I wasn't exactly popular trying to deny these older, more experienced guys an Olympic spot. Some were in their 30s, for heaven's sake, my age now, and were established internationals. There was a good camaraderie amongst the fleet but, at times, I felt a few of the older sailors were trying to intimidate me and bully me out of my chance on the water. My answer to this was to be just as aggressive back and that probably raised a few eyebrows. For sure, a few of the guys didn't like my aggressive style but, to me, when you were racing you committed your all, body and soul, and nothing else mattered.

I was no stranger to aggression and it was in some ways like it had been all those years before down in Cornwall when we'd knocked the hell out of each other. At least on the water. I couldn't care who I was up against. I was rock hard in my attitude. It was nothing personal. It could have been Prince Charles up against me, and I wouldn't have showed any respect. On shore, I was very different.

A couple of times it threatened to get out of hand. Some of us were training at Stokes Bay in Gosport at the time. There was a really helpful guy called Nick Harrison, who was from the slightly older generation of Laser sailors, and a stalwart of the club. He really took Iain under his wing, and to a certain extent myself. The environment reminded me slightly of the sailing club down in Cornwall.

One time down at Stokes Bay I came round behind this particular sailor. A complicated sailing manoeuvre was involved, but essentially he had the right of way round a mark, but once we'd cleared it, I had the right of way. I was quite aggressive and luffed this guy. We made contact, but he was in the wrong. He couldn't believe that I'd been that combative. I told him that I was going to protest and have him disqualified. When I got back to the beach, he actually went off and got one of his mates. The two of them grabbed me and had me pinned up against a wall. There was a lot of finger-jabbing. It didn't really bother me and I knew it was obviously getting to them.

People who had known me from my early teens knew I was incredibly committed and focussed. People who didn't know me up until then probably thought I was way too aggressive on the water. But I would only plead guilty to one charge: I cared too much.

To be honest, these things can happen in racing. It wouldn't be the last time, by any means, that I've provoked anger on the water. Fortunately, I had guys like Iain, Paul and Bart around so I wasn't the only young guy out there having a go. Iain was slightly more relaxed and chilled out than me, and would forever be smoothing things over. We'd have a laugh about that afterwards. Most importantly, the end result was that all my training in the winter paid off. I ended up winning the trials. It was a huge confidence boost.

So, what was the secret to success in those trials? I am not being immodest when I say that, in large part, it was because Mark Littlejohn and I had trained in Weymouth more than anyone else and had prepared better than anyone else.

We both moved to Weymouth and spent two winters training there solidly. We really went for it, were ferociously hard on each other. It took me back to the racing I did as a kid. In fact, Mark couldn't believe how aggressive it was, and how serious. We had a few arguments early on because of my approach. He'd try to calm things down and say 'What are you doing? We're just trying to train.'

But he was great. Mark understood my philosophy. That was: you've got to train like you race. He bought into that whole-heartedly. You've got to really try and push each other, and beat each other. That's the way you're going to get better. He really took that on board. We went out, just the two of us, no coach, and sailed against each other like it was a race. Obviously there weren't any marks as such. So, we'd race between the Russian trawlers which, at the time, used Weymouth as a base to anchor up and fillet their catch. Mark and I were out there through the winter, day after day, and I think that's what made the difference back then.

We did have a minor falling out a couple of days before the trials began. We had been out training, and I was behind him. But my strength, as is still the case today, is sailing downwind. If I didn't have a good first leg I could pass boats at that stage. Mark was never as quick as me downwind. That used to really irritate him. Mark had been trying to wind me up. So, as I sailed past him downwind, gybed around him and headed in, I called out, unnecessarily: 'See you later.' It must have irritated him and after that there was a tension between us, which was a shame. We'd both worked so hard. I suppose it was the pressure we were both under that made us so edgy.

Mark, Iain, Hugh Styles and I were the favourites for the trials, and there were about four or five other sailors who were also in with a decent chance. But Mark and I felt we had put in the most effort in terms of training. We felt we were the best prepared, but probably so did a lot of the other guys.

We went into the regatta. It was winner takes all. I started off really well. To demonstrate just how competitive it was, Iain and I came close in a race at the end of the second day, and there was an incident. Iain protested me. But Iain's your best mate, you may be thinking. To which I would respond: these *were* the Olympic trials. So, that's what he had to do. That's when you have to separate the racing from the shore side of things. But it can be difficult. As it transpired, his protest was dismissed.

By the final race, it was a head-to-head between myself and Hugh Styles. He'd also sailed a really good series, and was only two points behind me. He had to finish in the top five to beat me. Taking into account the discard system, it meant if I pushed him down the fleet, I'd end up winning, no matter what. It was not dissimilar to the strategy I would employ at Sydney five years later.

It was quite dramatic because we'd had a few days of no wind. The race was delayed. But we had to get this last race in, to ensure there was a series. It got later and later, and was six o'clock before the race started. I remember before the start looking over to Mark Littlejohn. Despite not really having spoken to each other for several days he glanced over to me and gave me a look that said: 'Go on, Ben. Go for it!' That was really a very sporting gesture. Mark had not had such a good regatta and so his Olympic dreams were over. It's such moments that you don't really forget.

Hugh Styles was a couple of years older than me and was a tough competitor but I felt I just had the edge. I thought to myself: 'This is it. I've got to take this guy down.' I took him out of the race. Just tacked on him all the way up the beat until we were last, all the way at the back of the fleet. One report said later that Hugh Styles and I 'completed a hundred tacks where just a dozen would be normal'. But crucially, Hugh was right behind me where I needed him. It was a four-lap race. At the end of the second leg I was still in front of Hugh. This was perfect.

But in sailing things rarely go completely according to plan. Nick Harrison, whom I've mentioned had been a real asset to Iain and me, had not been doing so well. He was also at the back. He had some boat-handling issues at the bottom mark rounding and I was forced to go outside him. He stopped his boat and I had to go even further outside him. Hugh, who was just behind me, nipped inside, and like a racing car at a chicane, overtook me.

I must concede I was panicking and gave Nick a hard time because he'd made the boat-handling cock-up that was causing me problems. The pressure was really on and by now it was almost dark. We had one more beat and the run to the finish to go. I just watched Hugh go for home, and prayed. He did a really good job, to be fair. He caught up a lot of places. But I had done enough. We were around six miles on the other side of Weymouth Harbour and we all had to sail back. That took an hour. By the time we got to shore it was about eight, and pitch black. It was bizarre sailing a dinghy in those conditions. But as we returned to the slipway, all I could hear was my dad yelling and cheering, and saying 'Well done, son. You made it.' It was a massive relief, although my delight was only temporary.

Yes, I had won the trials. But the selection panel still had to rubber-stamp my Olympic qualification, and there was an argument that, at 18, I wasn't experienced enough. I still had a long wait to have my selection confirmed. Eventually, the panel called me in and basically said that after seeing what I'd done to Hugh Styles in the last race they were pretty confident that I *did* have the experience.

I had done it. I had become the youngest ever British sailor selected for an Olympic squad. It was tough on Hugh and it was a testament to the way he had sailed all week that I had to use such aggressive tactics. You can't just ram someone or try and sink them. You have to do it within the rules. I have never been into cheating. But if you can slow a particular opponent down and keep them where you want them, it takes away the element of risk. It's not like track and field where a sprinter knows he can run 9.8 seconds, and the other guy isn't going to beat him because the best time he's done is 9.9. In sailing, you may be better than the other guy, but there's always the element of luck, and the wind plays its part. Normally, over a series that luck evens out. But if everything hangs on one race, then you've got to eliminate the risk.

What annoys me is that people talk about it being unfair. But to do that, you've first got to get yourself in front of the other guy. It's not as though you can just start in front of them and slow them down. It's actually quite difficult to do. People racing at that level also know it's coming and use strategies to avoid being caught out. I made it work against Hugh, and I learnt some valuable lessons. That was quite pertinent when you consider what the future had in store.

After my selection had been confirmed I went into the changing rooms for a shower, and there was Hugh – yes, it would be him – with head in hands. The poor bloke was just broken. What could you say? I just muttered: 'It was nothing personal. I just had to do it to win the event.' He didn't say anything, but I imagine he was thinking: 'Yeah. Right.' He hadn't made it that time, though he would go on to compete for Britain in the Tornado class at the Sydney Olympics.

He wasn't the only one not totally enamoured by my selection. In my wake I'd left a load of guys utterly deflated by the fact that they hadn't made it; a feeling exacerbated by the success of this 18-year-old. Somewhat bizarrely, at a time when I should have been celebrating, the notion suddenly hit me that I had a huge responsibility not to make a mess of the opportunity and let down all these guys who could have gone to the Games and could also have been successful.

What I did know was that I wouldn't just be going to Atlanta to take part. As Sir Steve Redgrave once said, if you don't travel to win, you're a tourist.

As a boy, I'd had many Olympic sailing heroes to take inspiration from. People like Mike McIntyre and Bryn Vaile who'd won gold in 1988 in the Star class; Rodney Pattison in the sixties and seventies, with two golds and a silver. In '92, I'd watched Lawrie Smith and his crew take a bronze in the three-man keelboat, the only British sailing medal at those Olympics.

From further afield, there had been the legendary Paul Elvström who won four golds at successive Games between 1948–60. As a kid growing up, I was particularly aware of the exploits of Russell Coutts, winner of the Finn in 1984. I'd heard about how Coutts never took any prisoners. He was out there to race and to win. That had a great influence on me and affected my attitude towards the sport.

As a child, you used to get people advising you: 'It's all about taking part.' At first, I probably went along with that. But after a time, I used to think 'Rubbish, I'm not interested in that. I'm there to win. If I'm not doing that, what's the point?' Quite often I'd hear people talking about having better luck next time but I always thought to myself, there may never be a next time. Maybe that's when I got that feeling that I had to start achieving things straight away.

For me, from the age of 15, sailing was never about participating. It was always about winning. I'd tasted success early on, in the youth worlds and other events, and I had enjoyed the feeling. People say winning is like a drug – and there's some truth in that.

But all the time I was learning what a tough sport it was, and how not everyone responded well to defeat. There was one race in the youth worlds which I won, but in doing so I got very close to one of the Aussie sailors when we were tacking up the first leg. There was a Portuguese guy who was close to me overall in the scores. He protested both me and the Australian, claiming that we'd hit, although we hadn't. At the protest there were three of us, and it was basically each man's word against the other. The protest was rejected, and nothing happened. I ended up winning, a German was runner-up and the Portuguese was third.

As we were standing on the podium, the Portuguese sailor said to me: 'How does it feel to have cheated and won?' I was so angry, I wanted to belt him. It was just an unbelievably crass thing to say at the time. Things like that happen in our sport. And it would be by no means the last time.

What sticks out for me in all sports at the highest level, is the how minute the increment can be between victory and coming second. Steve Redgrave can testify to that, of course. And, in football, any supporter of Chelsea – including myself – who watched the 2008 Champions League final, and witnessed John Terry slip as he missed his penalty in the shoot-out. After 120-plus minutes, it came down to that difference between the teams.

Some of my sailing successes have been on an absolute knife-edge. Sometimes I think back to the Olympics and world championships which I wouldn't have won unless I'd really gone for it and been totally committed to the cause. The difference at times was minute. There's plenty of really good sportsmen out there; many very good sailors. The difference is the determination to go that extra distance to win.

Perhaps it's partly in the genes. But I also put it down to racing David Lenz and Darren Williams in Cornwall in our Optimists. I was incredibly lucky to have those guys who were so tough to race. We had been so hard on each other. Something happened when we got on the water. We became . . . like machines. It got me familiar with that. From then, it was ingrained in me. I never felt bad about doing that. Other people would be shocked. But for me, ultra-aggressive sailing was just normal. That's how you should race. Once on the water, the gloves were off. But back on shore, we got on fine. We'd sit down and talk about moves and what had worked well.

David's still heavily involved in sailing, incidentally: He's a sail designer for North Sails, the biggest manufacturer of racing sails in the world, and a very successful big-boat sailor. Darren now runs his own IT business in London.

There's one other factor I can identify that contributed to my success. I was a worrier. In my teens, as I've admitted, I'd be anxious about all sorts of different things. Some were relatively trivial: scratching a car, money, and how I was going to pay for things. But the thing I was most paranoid about was fitness and being the right weight to race the very weight-sensitive Laser.

As I should have already mentioned, Iain Percy had finished fourth in those Olympic trials. He went off to university at Bristol. We still kept in close touch and a couple of times I went to stay at his place and we'd go partying with Goody and Bart. In some ways, I felt I was missing a period of my life not going through uni, but I was supposed to be training for the Olympics at this time and that was my sole focus.

I was so concerned about the effect of alcohol on my system that I'd come in at, say, midnight, one o'clock, and go running. It may sound strange, but it's the truth. I'd set off, pounding round the streets of Bristol in the early hours of the morning – purely because I felt really bad that I'd been drinking, and I had to go for a run to burn it off, get it out of my system. It sounds obsessive behaviour, but it's just the way I was, because I was so focussed on the whole thing. I was completely fastidious about not doing anything that would harm my fitness. If I didn't do that I'd feel really guilty. But by then, I was consumed by the prospect of the forthcoming Olympics.

Some young people don't care about anything. But I was completely the other way. Now, I'm far more relaxed than I used to be at 18. I'd like to say that I wouldn't dream of being so zealous now. Actually, that's not quite true. If I had a 'big' night I'd still go running the next morning. Purge my system. But, no, not in the middle of the night.

In the old days, when you could win events with a day to spare, which I managed a few times, you could go out celebrating because you've already finished racing, and have a few drinks. Strangely enough, I ended up racing pretty well the following day anyway . . .

I remember one European championship, in Helsinki, in 1999. I'd sailed well and I'd won the gold with a day in hand. It was Saturday night and a good mate, who hadn't had such a good regatta, suggested we go out and celebrate. We went into Helsinki, and had a long night. I got back at about 6 a.m. Being so far north, it was already light. Each day, I'd been running with my coach at 7 a.m. I came back, went into my room, put my running kit on, and came straight back out. My coach was there. He said: 'I can't believe you're up already, ready to go for a run.' I didn't have the heart to tell him the truth.

But that was all in the future. At this stage, I had more pressing matters: my first Olympics, as I entered four years that were to define my career.

Chapter 5

Outgunned by Scheidt in the Deep South

There was still a part of me that couldn't believe it. Qualifying for the Olympics at the age of 18 was incredibly exciting. Swimmers, gymnasts may make the big time virtually before they reach puberty. One of Great Britain's Beijing divers, Tom Daley, was only 14. But in sailing, a sport which really rewards experience, 18 is very young for someone to be taking on an Olympic Games. Yet, here I was, part of an Olympic sailing team in which there were so many characters I really admired. Coming out of the youth team, I was in awe of men like John Merricks and Ian Walker in the 470, and Glyn Charles in the Star class. At the time, I thought that was so cool. I really looked up to them and learnt a lot from just hanging out with them. Going up to London to be fitted out for the team kit was one of many things I had to do before travelling out to Savannah, where the sailing would be staged.

It was a strange feeling. I felt so confident, buoyed by what I'd achieved, but I also recognised that most people saw me as a bit of an enigma. Here I was, a young gun who'd arrived on the scene, seemingly so rapidly, and possessing something of a split personality. Most people just knew me as how I was on the shore: a bit shy but polite and unassuming. They couldn't equate that with my competitive demeanour once I'd set sail. I was like a piece of phosphorus. Normally controlled, but when exposed to certain conditions, liable to spontaneous combustion.

I have to say that the rest of the Great Britain sailing team were really supportive and embraced me. Some of the girls called me 'Baby Ben' which really pissed me off, but it was all good-natured. There was around a year between the trials and the Games, during which we had a team-building get-together in Dorset. At a team dinner, I was sitting next to an experienced sailor, Adrian Stead, who had been selected for the Soling class. A sponsor happened to come along, and said 'How do you think this guy's going to do?' Without hesitation, Adrian replied: 'He's going to win a medal – without a doubt.' I was still on a massive learning curve, and I knew I was getting better and better. But to hear him say that was a massive boost. They were really good to me, the whole team. I had won the spot fair and square. I was determined not to let down all these other more experienced sailors who had worked so hard for their places.

A lot of the team had already been out to the sailing venue at Savannah. I was aware that it was the kind of idiosyncratic sailing location that rewarded a lot of practice time, and getting thoroughly used to the conditions. It was a very open racecourse with a decent sea breeze but one that was quite shifty and tricky to read. The currents were strong as the Savannah River delta is a huge expanse of water. Also, due to the humidity there was a propensity for incredibly ferocious thunderstorms to let rip and blow out 30mph winds.

Of course, I'd never sailed there, and I decided that I needed to go out early and take part in the Fall Regatta in one of the RYA training boats. My dad came with me and the RYA arranged for us to stay at a house on Wilmington Island, owned by a lady called Karen Arms who had some involvement with the strong expat British community down there. Sailors were billeted with people who had volunteered to provide accommodation.

Dad and I arrived in the middle of the night, amid this massive thunderstorm. It was like a scene from a horror movie with trees swaying in the wind and a torrential downpour as we searched for the quiet suburb of Wilmington Island. The whole situation was somewhat bizarre. But remember, this was the Deep South, real redneck territory, with all the locals charging around in their pickups. To a British teenager, they were very strange people indeed.

Anyway, the next day I hired a Laser, and my father got hold of an old rubber dinghy to use as a coach boat. However, it took him two days to put it together in the searing heat. Meantime, I ended up training with some of the other foreign sailors who'd made the trip. It wasn't easy, though, as our training location, at the mouth of the Savannah River, was about twenty miles from the nearest marina. We went out on RIBs (Rigid Inflatable Boats) and took short cuts through the backwater, through the reeds. But it was stiflingly hot and humid, with lots of mosquitoes and insects which the locals had quite appropriately named 'no seeums'. And you had to watch out for alligators. Occasionally, there were the amazing thunderstorms. Like nothing you've ever seen.

Back in Britain, over the winter, my biggest problem was that I didn't have a training partner as the other sailors back home had rightly decided to take a break. All the guys in my event in

Britain had inevitably wound down after the trials, as winter approached. They'd been training for two years and hadn't made the team. Now they all had to get back to work or go to university. But I had to keep going. I still had a long way to go. I needed a top sailor to train against.

The solution was to go abroad. First, I went to Italy and trained with that nation's Olympic representative, Francesco Bruni, who'd won the world championships the year before. It suited us both. Francesco needed someone good to train against, too. He was based down in Palermo, and I stayed with him. We'd make the journey from his house through the streets to the sailing club on the back of his moped. He was a typical Italian where speed was concerned. It was just about the scariest moment of my life up to that date.

The Italians were clearly determined to put on a show to try and strike fear into me. Or that's what I could only assume. The routine was like this: we'd start off by running to the gym which was about six miles; we'd spend two hours there, then run back to the sailing club; then they'd cook up some pasta on the stove; then go sailing for about six hours in exceptionally strong, windy conditions – and I was in a borrowed boat, which wasn't in particularly good condition – before returning to do sprint training up and down the beach for an hour. It was unbelievably intense, physically. But there was no way you could ever sustain that punishing routine. We did five days of it. Fortunately, day six was a rest day. We both slept the whole day because we were so exhausted!

Those few days did have their benefits, though. I was still quite small at that time, with the consequence that I was good in light winds, and very good downwind. But not so good in strong winds. Though by now I was very proficient at boat-

Sailing at 5 years old

Steering our boat
Sule Skerry; it means
Seal Rock in Gaelic
and that's where
the boat ended up!

Dad (far right) and the crew of *Second Life* during the Whitbread Round the World race 1973-4

Dad teaching me how to steer to a compass heading. He was a great teacher, very patient

Mum helping Jim Saltonstall, the British coach, at the Optimist World Championships, Argentina 1992. Left to right there is me, Nick Rogers, Owen Ashton, Verity Slater, Jim, Chris Draper and Mum

With Dad, celebrating winning the 1999 Laser World Championships in Melbourne

Me trying to push Iain Percy back in the water at the Laser European championships in Sardinia in 1993. Iain was tenth in the full rig and I won the Laser Radial class

My nemesis and probably the best sailor I have ever raced against, Robert Scheidt

On the podium in Atlanta with Robert Scheidt of Brazil and Peer Moberg of Norway.
My first Olympics

The biggest race of my life. Taking on Robert Scheidt in the final race of the
2000 Olympics in Sydney

Mum and Dad watching the battle with Scheidt unfold from the banks of Sydney Harbour

Team GB putting sailing on the map in Sydney, winning 3 golds, and 2 silvers. With fellow sailing medallists Ian Walker, Mark Covell, myself, Iain Percy, Shirley Robertson, Ian Barker and Simon Hiscocks

(*Top*) The man who nearly stopped me winning my second gold medal in Athens – Guillaume Florent of France. He went on to win bronze in Beijing (*Above*) Taking a dunking after winning the second gold in Athens

The gym is an everyday occurrence. Contrary to popular belief, the sailors are as fit as the cyclists or swimmers

On the podium in Athens with my good friend Rafael Trujillo of Spain
and Mateusz Kusznierewicz of Poland

Surfing the waves on the way to winning gold in Athens

handling, I didn't have straight-line speed in strong winds because I wasn't big enough. In fact, that routine, with all the fitness training, was very good for me. By the time I left, I still couldn't believe how hard it had been. But if it was an attempt to demoralise me it didn't work. If anything, it had the opposite effect.

I then went to Holland for a week, and stayed and trained with the Dutch representative, Serge Kats. I found that he was the complete opposite. He barely did any training at all, and was incredibly laid-back. Serge was something of a hero of mine, having been two times Optimist world champion. He had also been third in the Laser world championships the year before; so, by now, not only was I learning from these guys, but I was getting a good gauge of the quality of the opposition.

Most significantly of all, as the British winter approached, I had received an invitation from the New Zealander Dan Slater, who had defeated me in the 1994 youth worlds but who had become a good friend. He invited me to stay with him in Auckland for two months, to train with him and take part in some big regattas down there, where the Kiwi sailors were preparing for their own Olympic trials. I seized the opportunity with relish. I went and had two and a half months of quality preparation. The good thing about New Zealand is that there is such a good balance between working hard and playing hard. We'd go to the gym in the morning, sail in the afternoon, and then go and have some fun.

That experience really improved me, and enabled me to work on my weak spot: developing my sailing in heavy weather. It set me up brilliantly for the whole of 1996.

And, so, I entered Olympic year in buoyant spirits. The world championships that year were in early March through to the beginning of April in Simon's Town which is just on the opposite side of the Cape of Good Hope to Cape Town. I stayed, appropriately enough, at the Lord Nelson pub which was run by a lovely Scottish lady who took me under her wing and made me eat like a horse. I was aware that Cape Town would be a really windy venue.

Some of the sailing we do is quite awesome in these smaller boats, the Laser or the Finn, which are only 12–14ft long. This was a good example. These were pretty ferocious conditions. Some sailors just freaked out. It was full on. I now love the strong wind conditions and the physical challenge that brings.

Halfway through those worlds, I was battling it out for the lead with Robert Scheidt and Karl Sunesson from Sweden. For me it was a step up to be challenging in that position. I had now become competitive, even in heavy breezes. That heartened me greatly.

Unfortunately, I got disqualified in one race because the clothing I was wearing was too heavy – by about ten grams. There is a weight limit of 8kg for clothing. In those days we all wore 4kg jackets and so that didn't leave much to weigh in under the 8kg total clothing allowance. It was really cold at that time of the year and I had taken an extra jacket from my coach between races. The second race of the day had restarted much quicker than I had anticipated and so I hadn't been able to offload the jacket before the race.

Frankly, that minute amount didn't make any difference but rules are rules. It was a tough hit to take but also a good reminder to try and stay on top of rules and measurement issues. It's easy to get slack and make a small error like that which can cost you big time.

The upshot was that the Brazilian icon, Robert Scheidt, won

the event, and deservedly so. I finished third, and was not far off being in contention for the lead. That was a huge boost. I regarded it as a great result in the conditions. Though Atlanta, now approaching rapidly, would be his first Games, Robert, who hails from a nation with a strong sailing heritage, was dominating the class.

As his name possibly suggests, he was actually of German-Brazilian background. He grew up in São Paulo and came from a wealthy family. He had sailed Optimists, as I had done, then he moved into the Laser, as I had too, and won the youth world championships. Robert was approaching the zenith of his career at this stage, having won the world championships in 1995 and now once again, in 1996. As I have said previously, I finished forty-second in 1994 and twenty-first in 1995, so I had a bit of catching up to do.

There was no doubt that he would be a tough adversary. He was so good, not just in the way he sailed but his whole approach: in his fitness and his total professionalism. He has always been a great athlete and he's very happy in that role of being number one, and though not in an arrogant way, he had become used to being lauded. I have to say he has always been a really good ambassador for the sport. I admired him greatly for that, together with his sportsmanship and trying to help the younger guys develop. At first, he couldn't have been more helpful to me. He'd happily offer advice as he passed on the water. 'Maybe you should try pulling that rope a bit harder,' he'd yell. That kind of thing. It was a great example to set. Admittedly, when I started becoming a threat to him, that all stopped. You couldn't blame him.

In hindsight, I'm convinced that without Robert's presence, I wouldn't have developed in the way that I did. If he'd been talented, but, not to put too fine a point on it, a pisshead who wasn't one hundred per cent committed but whose talent saw him through, then I could have been persuaded that you could get away with being like that too. But I knew I had to beat this guy who was not only an awesome sailor but also a magnificent athlete. It explains, in a way, why I'd go running in the middle of the night after any kind of alcohol consumption when I was younger. He's still the fittest guy I've ever met on the water. Robert was the complete professional, and I already knew that this was the guy I'd have to beat if I ever wanted to win anything. Some sportsmen spend their life thinking someone's unbeatable. That's never been my attitude.

While I have always respected him, I was aware from early on that he used his presence at the top of the fleet to intimidate people. Not in an unfair way. They'd just see him coming, and let him pass. But that was more the result of a psychological barrier that people created for themselves. Everyone's attitude would be: 'Oh, Robert, you're going to win. You're the man.' Everyone else in that Olympic cycle was racing for the silver. There were very few sailors who actually took him on and vowed: 'I'm going to beat you. *I'm* going to give you a hard time.' I sensed Robert didn't like that. He wasn't used to it.

That was his Achilles heel. He didn't like confrontation. If I was able to get him wound up, he wouldn't like that. Get him out of his comfort zone, and all of a sudden there were possibilities.

After the world championships, I went on to the Spa Regatta, finished six or seventh, and moved straight on to the European championships in June. That went like a dream. A few major Olympic contenders were missing, and Robert wasn't there, but I won by quite a big margin. I'd won the youth world championships and Laser Radial world championships but that was my first triumph in a major senior event. Going into the Games, that gave me the confidence that I could do really well. If I continued to sail at that level, I knew I could win a medal.

I went to Savannah, and trained for six weeks with my old training partner Mark Littlejohn who came out there. Also Hugh Styles came out and I was very grateful to both of them for their help and support. I could tell Hugh struggled with it and it must have been hard for him as he probably thought it should have been him out there preparing for the Games. It's one of the negatives with Olympic sailing that there is only one spot per nation. It means that a lot of seriously talented sailors never even get the chance to race in the Olympics. Hugh wasn't unique in the pain he probably felt. Iain Percy was also out there as a training partner for Richard Stenhouse in the Finn.

There was a training regatta three weeks before the Games at Hilton Head, South Carolina, a big beach resort, which was a bit like something out of Baywatch, with loads of Pamela Anderson-wannabe lifesavers in red bikinis. We sailed down there from Savannah, about fifty miles downwind, which was great fun and good practice time on the water.

Already I had discovered that sailing, being the really complex sport it is, can be hugely frustrating. It can push you to the limits, and far more than the uninitiated may suspect. Generally, I had made allowances for people, but then I ran into a French sailor named Guillaume Florent. He was something else altogether.

I first had experience of his excesses halfway through the training regatta series. Florent was leading the race. I started overtaking him on final leg to the finish. That was downwind, where, as I've said before, I was very quick. As I sailed past him, completely out of the blue he began screaming at me: 'You are f★★★★★★ cheating . . .' A barrage of bad language. I said nothing. The jury boat appeared. We had on-the-water judging, to make sure there was not too much rocking the boat and pumping the sails. Doing that to excess in light winds is not allowed under the rules and the judges are there watching you hawk-like.

The upshot of all this was that it was Florent who was given a yellow flag – for cheating! That meant him taking two penalty turns. As I went past, I laughed and yelled: 'I think you were the one who was cheating, mate.' At that point, he just exploded with fury. He absolutely went ballistic. He had turned into a complete psycho, and was virtually foaming at the mouth. I laughed, sailed off and won the race and thought nothing more of it.

I pulled up alongside a rubber boat, in which my coach John Derbyshire, my father, and Iain were waiting. But after the race the Frenchman came straight up, rammed us and tried to board the rubber boat. He had completely lost it. He was screaming things like: 'I'm going to kill you . . .' Fortunately, Iain Percy, who, as I say, had moved into the Finn by now, and had developed quite a big frame, just laughed and retorted: 'I don't think so, mate.' With four of us to contend with, including Iain, Florent thought better of continuing the row, and eventually sailed away.

Though a lot of the older guys were in general very supportive, it was good having such strong friends as Iain and Bart Simpson, and others of my generation around. When I first started out, we were the young guns. We all supported each other and stuck together.

At the end of the day, we got back to the beach and were packing things away. The next thing I saw was Florent and a New Zealand sailor sprinting towards each other and fists flying.

He'd done exactly the same to the Kiwi. It was unbelievable. I'd never seen anything like it. And it wasn't the last of our encounters.

Soon the Games themselves were upon us. Savannah, Georgia's oldest city, is 250 miles south-east of Atlanta – so we had no contact with the rest of the Great Britain competitors until we all travelled up to the closing ceremony. A very proud moment for me was the honour of being asked to carry the flag for the GB team at sailing's opening ceremony in Savannah. Rod Carr, who went on to become chief executive of the RYA, was then our team manager. I don't know whether it was a ploy by him to boost my confidence or not, but as the youngest member of the team Rod asked me to carry the flag. If I had one regret it was that we weren't at the main opening ceremony in Atlanta itself to witness Muhammad Ali, who had begun his career with a gold medal at the Rome Games of 1960, return to the Olympic arena to light the flame.

Our separate opening pageantry consisted of a parade along the waterfront in the centre of the city, followed by a little ceremony in a mini stadium on a lawn above the river. The old city was all old cobbled streets; an area which, apparently, pirates used to inhabit. There was loads of atmosphere. Typically for Savannah, known for its capricious weather, the heavens opened and it bucketed down. Everybody had to leg it back to the Marriott Hotel which the organisers had taken over and turned into an Olympic village for the sailors.

What do I remember about my introduction to the Olympics? Some odd things, like the hotel boasted a TGI Friday. And for us competitors, food came free. To a 19-year-old, that was a major plus about our facilities. The hotel also had a mini amusement arcade, with driving games. I was hooked on

Sega Rally at the time. I used to waste a lot of time on that with Hamish Pepper, the Kiwi representative in the Laser class, who was to become a good friend as well as a rival.

We tried to follow what was going on elsewhere in the Olympics by TV. Not that there was too much to cheer about from a British perspective. The most irritating thing was that we found being in the US there was only coverage of the sports which Americans were either any good at, or into: principally swimming, athletics and basketball. They didn't cover sailing, and they were certainly not into rowing, so we didn't see much of Steve Redgrave's and Matthew Pinsent's quest for gold. As far as Britain was concerned that was about it. Mind you, when you're competing at the Games you're so busy. Especially based in Savannah, where the daily schedule was exhausting.

The sailing course was a long way from the Olympic village. An old Sheraton Hotel, which used to be a mafia haunt, at the base of the river was used as the docking centre. There we boarded high-speed river boats which took you on a journey of around forty-five minutes to a sandbar at the mouth of the waterway. There they'd built a 'day marina' constructed of several barges which they'd taken down the river, anchored up and joined together. This temporary marina was twenty miles from civilisation and out in the wilderness, with just a cafe and offices for the race officials. It meant an extra hour commute on top of your day. Our competition days ended up being long and tiring, especially in the heat.

In Olympic sailing, our 'field of play' consists of five waterways, which define the courses that competitors have to compete in. These courses are indicated with marker buoys that are laid daily for the duration of the Games. Weather conditions play a decisive part. Every shift in wind strength or direction means that the buoys have to be repositioned. Committees at sea monitor the weather and lay the buoys accordingly. Normally, a race will take around an hour and a half. And there's no half-time, either.

The way that the scoring works in Olympic sailing is that the better your placing in each race the lower your points. Thus first place scores one point, second place two points, and so on. The winner is the competitor with the lowest aggregate score in all races, after the worst score or scores have been discarded. It meant that, in the old days, you could win with a day to spare. By 2008, that had changed. There was an opening series and a medal race on the final day.

But back to Atlanta, as I set out that first day, my first priority was to perform well, and show that my selection was not a mistake. Instead, it was an ignominious failure. In hindsight, it was crazy. I'd done a lot of training and raced there in the winter, but I'd never done a full race of an hour and a half in those conditions, in the summer heat out there. In training, I'd do half an hour and stop, and have a chat about it with John, my coach. What happened was that I had a terrible start, was mid-fleet, trying to catch up, and nearly passed out with heat exhaustion. I was in all sorts of trouble. I was burnt out. Physiologically, I wasn't properly prepared for it.

It was really bizarre. Maybe it was the pressure on me as well, but I almost had a physiological meltdown. My body could not cope with what was happening. It was a complete shock to the system. I remember finishing the race – I was somewhere down in the late twenties and my muscles were aching. I was so hot. I took down loads of fluid and was able to have a bit of a rest between races. As I did so, I reflected on the fact that certain people believed I was too young – remember, I had been only 18 when I qualified – and that my selection was a big mistake.

It was impossible not to have those thoughts. I knew I couldn't let them affect me. I tried to get them out of my mind as quickly as possible, and work out how to do better in the next race. The fact that my body had let me down was interesting. Six days a week for over a year I had prepared so hard for this event yet I had physically collapsed. Looking back, I think it must have been the consequence of the excitement of the occasion and the intense heat. But it wasn't good and it was another lesson learnt to go in the notes.

Fortunately, at that age my body adapted to those conditions more quickly than it possibly would today! By the second race of the day I had cooled off and recovered. I was able to pull through, and then go on from there. It went really well on the downwind leg. That was the really strong factor for me. It was always my strength. The conditions in Savannah gave you a real chance to make massive gains downwind, which I did. I remember I overtook a lot of boats, and finished in the top five, giving me a lot more confidence. I felt I was back on track, at least for the time being.

But the one thing I've learnt about the Olympics is to expect the unexpected. I arrived back at base to find I had received a protest from Florent, the French sailor. After what happened on the first occasion, maybe it shouldn't have surprised me. In the second race as we were approaching the first mark, Florent and I were very close when we were among twenty boats involved in an almighty pile-up. The poor American actually got T-boned by someone and his boat sank. Apart from him, we all managed to continue.

Normally, if you are going to protest somebody, you should declare it at the time. That gives the other sailor, if he accepts he is in the wrong, the opportunity to take penalty turns. Nobody said anything to me then, but when we got back to shore I looked on the protest list, and there it was: 'France protesting GBR'. 'What on earth was that all about?' I thought. There had been about twenty boats involved. It felt like it was a way to reduce my prospects in the regatta.

The protest meeting was held back at our Olympic 'village', the Marriott Hotel, and went on well into the night. Before we went in, the Frenchman sidled up to me and said: 'You know, I just had to do this because I had to watch my back. You should say that you were on port tack and I was on starboard tack.'

I will discuss the rules in more detail at a later stage, but it is important to know, in the context of this protest, that the boat on starboard tack, i.e. the boat with wind coming from his right-hand side, has the right of way if he is on a collision course with another competitor.

Florent is a bit older than me, and at the time, maybe thought I was completely naive and was setting me up for a fall. If he was then it was unbelievable. Anyway, I played along. We went into the protest room and he told the jury his perspective although it differed greatly from mine.

I told the jury what I saw; that I was on starboard, he was also on starboard, but another boat had come through on port.

We were sent out while the jury deliberated. As we waited, I noticed that, in the lobby of the hotel, there was a huge screen showing the day's racing. I happened to look across at the pictures. At that moment they showed the incident. It showed very clearly that I was the right-of-way boat. It was the complete opposite of what he had said. I went back into the jury room, and told them if they weren't sure, I'd just seen the incident on the telly. They went out, watched it, and it was exactly as I'd said it was. It was clear as day. Once the jury had looked at the video and deliberated, they found in my favour and I wasn't disqualified. But I was still annoyed. Though I left it at that, I felt the jury should have taken some action as our two accounts of the situation were vastly different. It was a pretty big pile-up, though, so I guess you could forgive the Frenchman for getting confused.

I was nervous that first day for sure. I don't think you'd be human if you didn't show some nerves; either that or you don't care enough. I think the answer to nerves lies in the preparation. There's an old saying, 'The harder you train the luckier you become.' If you have trained as hard as you can and done the right preparation then that's all you can do. From there on, it comes down to racing well and focussing your energy on racing, not worrying about what you could have or should have done beforehand.

From the following day, I sailed a blinding series. A couple of times I was maybe a little bit lucky. There were quite a lot of thunderstorms, some of them approaching biblical proportions, and in a couple of races when I wasn't doing so well, I saw the storm coming and made the right tactical decision. Importantly, I was able to get on the right side and come through those races unscathed, whilst around me there were some pretty big wipeouts.

I started getting a sequence of really good results: first and second places for the next five races. From a desperate start, I forged into an overall lead.

That's when it started getting a little bit difficult with Robert. We were quite a long way ahead of the rest of the fleet. He started giving me a hard time. The final three races of the series were about Robert and I trying to wrench the initiative from each other.

Apart from Robert, who was sailing really well, as I could have anticipated, just about everyone else was falling by the wayside apart from the Norwegian, Peer Moberg. It ended up with the pair of us going into the last two races virtually neck and neck. It was then that he really rankled me. It took four years to get over it. Robert was older and fitter and stronger and faster than me, especially upwind. We both had good starts in the penultimate race, but he was quicker. Robert tacked on me a few times to put me right at the back of the fleet. He was at the front.

It was a defining moment in my career. I was so determined to get back and overtake him, I dug really deep and found something within me to get me back up the fleet. In one leg, downwind, I overtook about fifteen boats to round the bottom turning mark right behind him. I knew he'd wanted to get me out of the running as I was the main threat but I thought it was too early to be playing these games. Maybe I was wrong. I was so frustated he had given me a hard time, I was screaming at him in anger. I don't know if he heard, but I was pretty fired up by this point.

It was the best I'd ever sailed, to overtake the whole fleet and get up behind him. Then overtake him. We ended up at the windward mark together, and hit each other. We both did penalty turns. About five boats overtook us. Then we were off again, and we passed the fleet. He won the race and I was second. It was really bizarre. Something inside me clicked. It had become personal.

We went into the final race, and Robert used his experience and turned a potentially devastating mistake into a gold medal-winning outcome. I needed to beat Robert by five places to win gold. We'd both been messing around with each other before the start, trying to get an upper hand. I went to start more towards the middle of the line. Robert went near the committee boat, at the end of the line, where they do all the signalling. You can hear a lot of what is being said from the committee boat. There had already been one start which had been recalled. Then after that they hoist a black flag for the starting sequence. That means that, from then, if anyone is over the line in the last minute before the gun goes, that boat is disqualified. Even if the fleet is recalled again, he is still disqualified from the race.

Robert was near the committee boat, and drifted over the line. He must have heard them call his country name. At that point, he knew he was out of the race, regardless. Crucially, I wasn't aware of that. Nor was anyone else. What he did was very smart. With five seconds to go, he just sheeted in and went for it. He was yards over the start line before the gun went. But that triggered a whole group of us, about ten to fifteen boats, to go as well. If you see someone going, you don't want them to get a jump on you. I was disqualified as well. It was a great move by him but quite ballsy. If he hadn't got away with it, he'd have been out of the race, and I'd have had a good chance of taking the gold but I knew I had to have a good race, and had to go for it.

I had been experienced enough not to fall for ploys like that perpetrated by the French sailor Florent at the earlier protest. I shouldn't have fallen for Robert's at this crucial moment, either. Today, I wouldn't get myself in that position on the start line. I probably would handle it differently. I learnt a lot from that. It helped me in future. In general, I'm pretty good at learning from my mistakes.

A lot of sailing is about mental rehearsal, making a mistake and working out how you could have done it better. And next time, you do it better. I've done so many races now where each situation I come to I've got a mental picture of what happened before and what didn't work, and it helps you make the right decision. It takes a lot of time to build that up. You can spend hours studying the theory on white boards. But until you do it in practice, you don't get that same mental picture that you get from real experience.

If I could rerun that final race at Atlanta, things would have been decidedly different. As it was, I had to console myself with a silver. It wasn't easy. At the time, I was devastated.

Chapter 6

Breaking Robert Scheidt's Spell

It took me about half an hour to sail back to the day marina, and that gave me time to reflect. My overriding emotion was real disappointment not to get the gold. Back then, you wonder how many chances you are going to get to compete in an Olympics – and how many opportunities to win a gold medal. I'd come really close, but hadn't made it. That was very frustrating. It seems stupid now. But I couldn't erase the thought from my mind that this may be my only chance in an Olympics. I'd had a really good chance to win the gold, and let it slip. I was so disappointed, even though, with the benefit of not really having had the pressure of expectation on me at all, I had achieved a really good result. It had been a great experience.

If I'm ultra-critical, I probably got a little carried away by the whole Olympic experience. I was a bit wide-eyed, and maybe just lost some focus on the racing. But overall I had sailed well.

Yet still the outcome irked me. So near, and yet so far. I had never believed I had come to the Games just to compete for its own sake. I've always been a big student of the sport and its history. I'd even confess to being a bit geeky. I could probably tell you who the bowman was in some race in 1980. I've always watched videos of old Olympic Games, read copiously about the gold medallists. It was always my ambition to try to emulate some of these people. So, for me, it was always the case that qualification for the Olympics was about trying to win a medal, preferably a gold. I wasn't really interested in the blazer or the badges. Sure, those things were a novelty then, and exciting. But they weren't what it was about.

As I've said previously, you constantly hear this old adage that it's not about the winning, but about the taking part. I must stress that I fully agree this is the right message to give to young people starting out – that they should enjoy it first and foremost. But to me, as soon as I took it seriously as a career, then it was all about winning. I wasn't interested in anything else.

Only gradually did I accept that, as one experienced sailor told me when I returned home, failing to win the gold was 'probably the best thing that could have happened to you'. Deep down, I knew that I still had a lot to learn, and a long way to go.

After being disqualified in that finale, I had stayed out to watch the race take place. Robert Scheidt had no need to do so. He sailed straight back in, because he knew he'd won, regardless. I couldn't even be certain that the silver was mine. If the Norwegian competitor, Peer Moberg, had done really well, he could have relegated me to the bronze position, and the feeling would have been even worse. Fortunately he didn't.

After Robert and I had been disqualified from the last race, Moberg had sailed up to me and said: 'Thank you very much. Now I can win the silver medal.' I didn't think it was a particularly sporting thing to say. To my amusement, he went on to sail a terrible race and had to settle for bronze.

When I returned to the dock, it was great to see some friendly faces although only a few people were allowed on to the day marina. I received a great response from my teammates and that meant a lot, because there was still a residue of disappointment within me; still a feeling lingered that I'd somehow let everyone down. That reception lifted me. I suddenly started to feel a bit better about things. I came to realise that winning a silver at that age was really some achievement. It took me a while to go through drug control, before meeting up with my parents, who had been out on the spectator boat. They had watched the racing with Robert Scheidt's parents, of all people. The four of them actually got on really well.

At that age, to have my parents out in America supporting me was really crucial. Not that I had spent too much time with them. I was busy being dragged around doing interviews, and felt really bad because there was so little time to see them. They had put in so much effort into helping me get so far, and probably felt they deserved more attention. They and Fleur had rented a place out there since well before the start of the Olympics.

The non-sailing media had materialised, in part because there wasn't really very much going on anywhere else. That's what happens at Olympics. The British press, like prospectors in the Old West, congregate wherever there may be gold. With no sign of a medal rush back in the Atlanta area, there was a realisation that there were some sailors doing well, with a chance of gold, elsewhere in Georgia. The non-sailing media's arrival was something of a shock because, up to then, we had been in our own little world. We had definitely felt cut off from the rest of the Games in which the dominant figure had been the American, Michael Johnson. He had proved himself an outstanding sportsman by becoming the first athlete in history to win both the 200m and 400m at a single Olympics, and went on to add a third gold medal in the 4 × 400m relay. Those Games will, sadly, also be remembered as those when a terrorist bomb in the Centennial Olympic Park killed one spectator and wounded 110 others.

Despite the British optimism created by three previous Olympics, just one gold medal-winning performance by the coxless pair, Steve Redgrave and Matthew Pinsent, was a major disappointment overall.

It was felt that many British athletes had underperformed. Fortunately for Great Britain, Redgrave and Pinsent, undefeated in fifty-eight races stretching back to 1992, had prevailed in their final – the victory making Redgrave Britain's most successful Olympian, with his fourth straight gold medal in as many Games. It prompted that famous quote: 'If anyone sees me near a boat again, they have my permission to shoot me. I've had enough.' He did return, of course.

For myself, I had every intention of getting back into a boat, with the determination to improve on that silver next time.

No doubt, many people assumed I would have been satisfied to prove something to my peers, and particularly those who had questioned my experience. But other people's perceptions of me were irrelevant. In all honesty, that's not something I have ever dwelt on – which is possibly one of my strengths. I simply concentrate on my own development, not others' opinion of it. When I started with Optimists, I quickly climbed the ladder. And that also happened in my Laser career. I'd won a youth world championships; that same year I qualified for the Olympics; and now I'd won a silver. Next step was a gold.

To have pushed Robert Scheidt so hard confirmed my swift

progression as an international sailor. As I've observed already, others were prepared to be intimidated by him. I had shown him I was not like that. I had failed narrowly, but vowed to put it right in the future. It was the start of probably the most intense period of my life, from then until Sydney.

I had sensed throughout the racing a feeling not exactly of fear, but an underlying acceptance throughout the fleet, that Robert was unbeatable. I felt very strongly that I could break the spell he had seemingly cast over the class. Indeed I had to do so if I was to win gold in 2000. That would be my focus in the intervening years.

Fitness would be my priority. I can't stress enough how important that is. It's one of the misapprehensions about race-sailing. People often think it's a technical sport, when, in fact, it's highly physical. We wear heart-rate monitors when we're racing, and when it's windy your heart rate will be peaking at 195. You'll be in that zone of 165–195 beats per minute for up to half an hour. You're really pushing yourself. Sailing in strong winds, fitness is eighty per cent of the game in terms of your result. You see guys who started off well in a race, but by the end they're tired. They either start making mistakes, and capsize, or their boat-handling lets them down. Or they just don't go so quickly because they're not working the boat so hard.

My style has always been very physical in the boat, especially when it's windy. You'll see lots of dynamic movement, with trimming of the sheets to keep the boat moving perfectly around the waves. That requires a lot of strength and stamina. It's a huge part of being successful and controlling the boat in the strong winds.

When I was younger, I had worked hard on conditioning myself. Though I probably thought I was fit enough, in reality I wasn't. It meant I suffered from a lack of endurance. Mine didn't compare, at that time, with that of Robert Scheidt, who was, as I've said, an incredibly tough and resilient opponent. It took me until I was maybe 22, 23 to finally get that level of fitness.

Fitness is something everyone can address. Not all possess the necessary self-belief.

I was aware that, even then, I was developing a reputation for single-mindedness, though I was a real Jekyll and Hyde character. Off the water, I was very shy. I probably didn't have much self-confidence. I'd worry and worry, and waste ridiculous amounts of time fretting about whether I'd done things right. Was I training hard enough, preparing myself correctly? Yet, once I got on the water, something within me changed. It was as though I had downed a potion that brought about a transition in my character. There was nothing I did that changed my mental state. For whatever reason, I just switched on. It was the racing that transformed me.

Back then, on the shore, I wouldn't say boo to a goose. On the water, I was supremely self-confident. I was a totally different person. I had the confidence to tell some 30-year-old guy who'd won numerous world championships where to stick it. It's kind of scary now, when I think back to it. I guess it really came from a desperate desire to win, and be successful.

Returning to the immediate aftermath of my Olympic debut, the medal ceremony, on 3 August 1996, took place in the mini stadium in Savannah that they'd set up by the side of the river. As I stepped up to the podium to receive my medal, I glanced to the right. The whole of the British team were there. They all stood up, applauded and cheered, and made a massive fuss. That really touched me a lot. I hadn't seen much of anyone else in the previous few days, because they had been concentrating hard on their own events. John Merricks and Ian Walker had won a silver in the 470. At one time, it hadn't looked as though Britain would win a medal at all in the sailing, so there was considerable relief all round, I recall, that we'd achieved what we had. As a team we'd performed strongly considering how the rest of the GB Olympic team had done. That night a few of the top men at the BOA came down and took us all out to dinner in the old town. The precis of the message was: 'Thank God for sailing!'

Personally, I'd had a fantastic year, but I definitely felt I had to go on to the next level, and take on Robert Scheidt and beat him.

Initially he had been helpful, but that attitude changed a little bit after it became obvious that I was becoming his main threat. He wasn't quite so friendly. When I received the silver, he was very sportsmanlike, very complimentary. To be fair, he had been the better sailor and deserved to win. I congratulated him, as you should. But silently I was already scheming how I was going to beat him next time round. Let me emphasise, particularly in view of what would occur in four years' time, that I didn't dislike Robert. I had a huge amount of respect for him. I was just one hundred per cent committed to trying to beat him. That was all I wanted to do.

You try and have a good relationship with everyone. There's strong camaraderie in sailing. But you rarely get close to the guys who you know are your main competition. There always has to be that distance. Having said that, there are a few rivals I've always been friendly with; in particular, some of the Kiwi sailors. I've made some great friends over the years. And, of course, Iain Percy and Bart Simpson have been really good mates, even through times when we were racing each other. It's always easier to hate the competition when you're out on the water.

Two days later, we went by coach up to Atlanta. We spent a day there, went round the Olympic village and met individuals like Linford Christie, Steve Redgrave and Matthew Pinsent. Then it was on to the closing ceremony. It was there that I got together with my first real girlfriend, Boel. She was a Swedish 470 sailor, and we'd actually first met back in Savannah after racing had finished. We had chatted, and I wanted to see her again. The trouble was that I didn't have a phone number (this was before everyone had a mobile, and before texting) or any contact details. As it happened, fate intervened. In those days, all the athletes were in seats in stands and at the end of the ceremony piled on to the track. There were thousands of people, but somehow I managed to find her. It was quite an achievement.

We met up again in New York later that summer, and were together for around nine years. It was long-distance for a couple of years, then we lived together for quite a while. She was a great girl, slightly older, which was a good thing as she managed to stop me going off the rails, which I guess as a teenager was always a possibility. One of the very few drawbacks of being a sailor is that it's incredibly hard on relationships of any kind. Disappearing for up to three months at a time doesn't normally go down too well with partners, and like in any other sport, that degree of single-mindedness can often be very hard to live with for the other person. It's frustrating at times as often you just crave a normal life – but then to have so many amazing opportunities I regard myself as very fortunate.

After the Games, my arrival home was a slightly surreal experience. Of course, I had an Olympic silver medal in my hand baggage and I felt a sense of achievement. But there was also a sense of emptiness. I received an invitation to Downing

Street to meet the then prime minister, John Major. I was quite impressed by him. For a start, he actually knew my name. Not all politicians are as well prepared, I can assure you. I took Dad with me. I remember being very impressed at finding members of the England football team there too, following the fine performance of Terry Venables' men at Euro '96. They included Gazza, wearing a loud check suit, and accompanied by a minder.

I suppose, at that age, I quite enjoyed that brush with celebrity. I also danced on stage with the Spice Girls, who were very big at the time, on the *National Lottery TV Show*. That was exceptionally embarrassing because I can't dance at all. It was one of those bizarre things you end up doing. And, no, I can't say I was a fan . . .

But that couldn't alter the fact that there was this massive void in my life. Initially, I stayed at my parents' home, but I had no real plans. I went to see some friends who were doing the national championships in the Laser class up at Swansea, stayed with them for a while, and then came home. I thought: 'What do I do now?' With another four years stretching ahead of me, I didn't really have any immediate motivation to start training again straight away. It was a really odd feeling.

Beforehand I hadn't given it a thought. The Olympics were my horizon, and nothing lay beyond.

So, after a weird couple of weeks I decided that I should finish off what I'd begun, and complete my A levels. I enrolled at Peter Symonds College, which was where I had been for a year and half previously, but had left to train for the Atlanta Games.

I simply couldn't make the transition back. I'd just had the experience of being absolutely focussed for the Olympics and making every minute count. Now, after being away for a year, and growing up a hell of a lot in that time, I returned to college and found myself sitting around in a classroom for half an hour while the teacher had to argue with some idiot who hadn't done his homework. It infuriated me. I thought to myself: 'This is just a waste of time. I don't have the time in my life to be doing this.' I looked at the college timetable and my sailing schedule, because by now, I had begun looking ahead to Sydney 2000 and realised there were some pretty big clashes there. Someone suggested a tutorial college in Winchester. So, I transferred to that and did my A levels there instead.

It was the best thing I ever did. It cost me some money, but I was able to fit the lessons around my training schedule. My reward was two grade Bs, in Business Studies and Environmental Science. For me, it was quite important to tick that box. It was a definite omission in my life. At least it gave me the option to go to university and study for a degree if I decided it was something I wanted to do, and have that base covered.

I suppose there was also a sense of pride. Some of my friends, people like Iain Percy, were at university and studying for degrees. In a way, I felt a bit inadequate.

Yet, already, even before 1996, I knew that sailing was what I wanted to do as a career. I never considered anything else. It would have been great to have gone to university, but I just don't think I could have fitted it in. Not with the other priority I had: overcoming the might of my nemesis, Robert Scheidt.

Chapter 7

Sydney on the Horizon

The climax of my determination to fracture Robert Scheidt's Olympic pre-eminence in the Laser class would come in one race, on one day, in August 2000. Yet, in fact, it was the culmination of three years' preparation.

Know your location. It is a crucial dictum in sailing. For me, it was as true of Sydney as it had been of Atlanta. I spent as much time as I could down there, training and racing. From three years before the next Olympics, test regattas are staged by the hosts. I won those at Sydney in 1998 and 1999, both in August: the same time of year as the Games were going to be held. That was a good confidence boost at the same venue. I felt I was really getting a grasp of the conditions as I set about the task which had become an obsession.

I was galvanised in everything I did by the desire to beat Robert. Not winning in 1996 had given me all the incentive I needed. It was a stark, ever-present reminder that I still had another level to ascend if I was to reach the zenith of Olympic achievement.

I first travelled out to Sydney in 1997, to check it out. I'd never been there before. My first impression of sailing in the harbour was how beautiful it was, and what a great city it was. Then we actually started racing. You imagine it being relatively benign. The perfect location. In fact, Sydney Harbour is one of the hardest places to sail. It's a bit like sailing on a giant version of the Thames. The huge buildings and the very hilly topography contrive to make the wind incredibly fluky. And there's quite strong currents, too. In all, its waters are something of a nightmare to race on.

And that's before you have to negotiate the harbour traffic. The Manly ferry is infamous in sailing. In most harbours you go to, sailing boats have the right of way, whereas in Sydney Harbour the ferries have priority. They *will* mow down boats. They won't change their course. They don't care. It's incredible. So, that was a big part of the day; making sure you didn't get run down by a Manly ferry.

There were four courses inside the harbour and two outside the 'heads' or out to sea. In the Laser class we only ever raced inside the harbour and so the big issue was trying to acquaint yourself with the different areas of this amazing stretch of water. It was like a massive strategy board game. Each of the headlands and islands had their own little tidal eddies and wind-shifts and so it was a case of working out the best course, taking full advantage of the harbour and its nuances.

It took me a while to familiarise myself with those surroundings. The first event we all competed in was the Sydney International Regatta, known as the SIR, in November 1997. Robert Scheidt won, I finished second. The conditions made one race a real ordeal. I remember losing my cool completely, and after the race going up to John Derbyshire, my coach for the 1996 and 2000 Olympics, and saying: 'This is absolutely ridiculous. They can't possibly hold the Olympics here. These conditions are a complete joke.'

John looked me in the eyes and retorted: 'There are two things you can do. You can keep moaning about it, and get upset. Or you can realise that they are going to hold the Olympics here. There's nothing you can do about that. You'll either take it on, and learn how to sail in these conditions and see it as a challenge. Or you may as well pack up and go home because the harbour has been here a lot longer than you have.'

That was great. I needed him to say that and I had to embrace it, and take it on. I did, and from then on I really enjoyed sailing in Sydney Harbour. I took it as a real challenge, to learn to sail in those conditions and be good at it. And that's probably what helped me to win.

Your coach plays a major part in any victory – even in the Laser, which is a very simple, straightforward boat to sail and campaign. You don't really need any assistance in terms of setting up the Laser, compared with the Finn, which I moved on to, and which I'll come to later. The Laser is a standard design. If you want to sail one in, say, Mexico next week, you can go there and get one that's exactly the same as one you'd sail here. You need to be a good self-coach, in terms of analysing your weaknesses.

At the very top level, having a coach is more about having someone to talk to; a mate more than anything, with whom you can have a chat about things. In some ways, it's a case of the sailor leading the discussion rather than the coach sitting you down and saying you did this, or that, wrong.

There are also practical reasons to have a coach on race days. He makes sure you get food and drink between races, tows you out to the course if there's no wind, and carries spare equipment. He will also help with weather forecasting and to run the training sessions before any big regatta. We use a lot of video analysis in sailing and John was also very keen on that. More often than not your coach will be catering for more than one guy in the squad so it can be tricky at times, but at the Olympics it's normally just one on one.

John had actually been appointed Olympic team manager for 2000, and that made life quite difficult for us, because he was busy running the sailing team as a whole. That led to a few issues. On the penultimate day of the series we were due to race on one of the courses furthest away from Rushcutters Bay which served as the Olympic sailing and sailboarding base.

John was busy but I arranged to start sailing out to the course and he would meet me as soon as possible and tow me the rest of the way as the wind was light. After half an hour, there was still no John. I was starting to get worried that I'd miss the start of the race. In fact, he had gone out in his RIB and somehow missed me as he rushed to get out to the course area and, by now, was on his way back. We eventually made contact, and I can look back now and laugh about it, but at the time I was pretty stressed. At that rate I was only just going to make it to the course on time, but fortunately due to the light airs the race was postponed and catastrophe was averted.

Sailing's administration rightly gets held up to other sports as an example of how it should be done. That's partly down to continuity. For the past thirteen years, it has been largely the same guys running the sport; notably Rod Carr who has had several key roles in sailing and is currently CEO of the RYA. John Derbyshire is still heavily involved as the head of the racing division, and Stephen Park, or 'Sparky' as we all know him, has risen through the ranks to become the Olympic manager. That's really important, in terms of developing each Games we've competed in; not just from a management point of view, but in terms of the set-up and logistics, what works and doesn't work. Both the sailors and the management have learnt from each Olympic experience and it is now a pretty well-oiled machine, but that doesn't mean there aren't issues from time to time and that we can afford to sit back and relax. Like all other Olympic sports, sailing relies heavily on funding from UK Sport and the National Lottery, as well as team commercial sponsors and, of course, funding is very much reliant on getting results.

Talk to people in other sports and the RYA is rightly regarded as a very good governing body. Of course, there are things we don't always agree on and someone like myself is always prone to having a very elitist attitude. It can be frustrating, but it's not just about me and what I want. When you're at the Olympics it's about the whole squad and you really just have to make slight adjustments to run your campaign around a larger team environment. As sailors we benefit from having such a strong governing body but they are also fortunate to have had a generation of sailors who have gone out with the determination to succeed. I think we have to be careful that in the modern era of Olympic sports we don't try and mould kids from a very young age into what we think will be a future Olympic champion. It has to be about giving youngsters the right support but also letting them take full responsibility for their careers.

Returning to my preparation for Sydney, I mainly sailed out of Woollahra Sailing Club at Rose Bay, in the eastern suburbs of the city, a really nice area. As I've explained, there were four different course areas within the harbour, and I'd train in one for maybe a couple of hours, then alternate to another to break things up. One day, I was training on my own and I thought it would be quite cool to sail from Woollahra round to Bondi

Beach, Sydney's iconic surf beach – and try to see if it was possible to surf a Laser.

One of the most famous stretches of sand in the world, a magnet for surfboarders, swimmers and sunbathers, and, of course, those lifeguards, the name is apparently derived from the Aboriginal. Bondi means 'place of breaking or tumbling waters'. I can testify to the fact that it is an apt description.

I went in on what was relatively quite a small set of waves, and thought 'This is pretty good, I'm happy with that.' But I turned round to come back and a really big set of waves came in and I just got to the wave before it started to break. I went up on this wave, and the boat was actually airborne. It slammed down hard, and I was so close to flipping; if that wave had got me I'd have just gone over backwards and I'd have been wiped out on the beach. The boat would have been destroyed – and I'd have looked pretty average walking up the beach with a smashed-up Laser behind me.

I didn't push my luck any more. I returned to Woollahra, which is quite a long sail round. It's about two hours. On the way, a couple of inquisitive sharks glided up alongside. It was quite windy as well. 'Hmm,' I thought, 'better make sure I don't capsize . . .'

Spending a lot of time training out in Australia, and New Zealand too, was valuable for another reason: both nations have reputations of placing a strong accent on winning. It's part of their culture. I have spent a lot of time over there. As I said earlier, in the build-up to Atlanta I had done winter training in New Zealand. I stayed in Auckland and trained with Dan Slater. It made a huge difference. I made a great leap forward. I took a lot from their training and work ethic, the racing that they did, the way they sailed, their focus. Also, in Britain, we tend to race in the summer from March to November. When it got cold, people would pack it in for four months over the winter.

Sure, the climate helps down there. But in Britain – I'm sorry to say this, but it's true – a lot of people have a strange attitude towards sport. We're very good at excuses for not winning. I found that was true in sailing, particularly from the generation before me. Now you don't see it so much and we have a much more positive attitude. Success breeds success. But back then, it was always 'Oh, the equipment wasn't right', or 'We didn't have enough money', or 'I was really unlucky'. But Kiwis and Aussies don't do excuses. If you've always got an excuse, you never really get to the crux of the problem about why you're not doing well. You've got to be honest and realistic with yourself.

I can candidly admit that 1997 was not my finest racing year. I lost the European championships down in Cascais, Portugal. In the final race of the series I took the wrong course. It was nobody's fault. Basically a marker had drifted, and a whole group of us who had blasted off into an early lead, went the wrong way. Sometimes you barely have time to think. If it's very windy, as it was then, and there's a danger of capsizing, you have to focus on that. You have to make instant decisions. By the time we'd realised that we'd got it wrong, we looked around to see all the rest of the fleet, who had been behind us, miles ahead in the distance. Right then, we knew that we had blown it. I protested the race committee, on the basis that the marker was in the wrong place. But the protest was thrown out and I lost the series.

The beneficiary of all this was none other than Hugh Styles, who had lost out to me in those Olympic trials before Atlanta. He had sailed a great series and took full advantage of the mistake we made up ahead in the leading pack. Hugh ended up winning the championships and I was third. It was a pretty tough way to lose an event. I think Hugh obviously felt pretty good about it and certainly made the most of his time on the podium.

The 1997 world championships in Chile were another bad event for me, but for more than the obvious reason. While I was out there training, the forthcoming regatta was all over-shadowed for me by the shocking news that John Merricks had been killed in a car accident. John, who had won a silver in the 470s in Atlanta, was one of sailing's nice guys and an extremely talented sailor. A bit older than me, he had always been a good friend. It was a real shock. My natural inclination was to go straight home and attend the funeral. I spoke to my dad about it. He insisted: 'I'm sure John would have wanted you to be out there racing; he wouldn't have wanted you to miss the world championship.' So, with some reluctance, I stayed on.

Once I got into the racing, I wasn't quite quick enough, anyway. Halfway through I wasn't doing that well at all, but came good towards the end, and eventually finished third overall. I was a bit frustrated, particularly as Robert Scheidt won again.

Out in Chile, I tried a couple of times to give Robert a hard time. In the first race we were involved in an incident, in which I was quite aggressive. Probably too aggressive. I was pushing it a bit, but essentially he was in the wrong, and he had to do penalty turns. He wasn't happy about that. I remember we had some quite harsh words after the race. He told me: 'If you keep sailing like that then you and I are going to fall out.' In hindsight he was probably right.

There was another race, the second to last, when we were locked together, within two boat-lengths of each other, all the way round the course, and I held him off right the way to the finish. We were miles ahead of the rest of the fleet. It was very windy. And it was all about fitness. We were neck and neck the whole way. He tacked. I put in a classic tack just in front of him. He reached underneath me. Towards the finish, it was straight-line sailing. I've never worked so hard in my life. I just got across the line in front of him. How hard we pushed each other. I felt dead at the end of it.

That was some encounter. It stands out as one of the best racing experiences I've ever had. The trouble was that he won the world championships by finishing second in the race. Robert deserved it. He had sailed a brilliant series again.

The important aspect was that I had relished the conflict. I knew that if I was going to beat Robert I was going to have to sail at one hundred per cent. When I look back now, I regard that period as involving the most intense racing, at an elite level, that I've ever had in my life. Fantastic. When I'm old and grey and reclining in my armchair, I will still remember such races as my greatest challenge.

I had beaten Robert in a few regattas that year but not the big ones and I knew I had to do better.

I sat down with John Derbyshire, and we talked about areas to improve. Fitness was one of them. I knew I still needed to work harder on the endurance side of things.

Physique was something I'd always struggled with. I was naturally lighter than Robert, who's also quite a tall guy. That means he's got more leverage when he's leaning out of the boat. It was initially quite hard to keep up with him when it was windy. If you set out to design the ultimate dinghy sailor, it would probably be Robert. He's about 6ft 2in, very fit and very skinny. That's really perfect for the Laser. For the optimum performance, your weight's got to be right, in the range of 76–81kg. I was always more towards the bottom of that range in my younger days; Robert more towards the top of it. That said, it was always my choice to be slightly lighter, because I felt it made me more competitive.

During that year, 1997, I concentrated on continual training and development, and trying to get fitter and stronger. I focussed on specific areas. As I've said previously, I was very good downwind. But sailing upwind when it was windy, I really struggled for straight-line pace. And reaching (sailing with the wind abeam, which is approximately at right angles), I was OK, but not that good. I began working again with Mark Littlejohn. He helped me to improve on those two areas. That got me to the level, speed-wise, where I was equal to Robert Scheidt.

In 1998 my results improved considerably. I won the European championships in Austria, so that gave me a lot more confidence. And then I finally beat Robert at world-championship level. For me, that was really significant. It was in Dubai, which is a slightly lighter-wind venue, and that suited me eminently. My reward for these two victories was to be voted the ISAF (International Sailing Federation) World Sailor of the Year which was a huge honour.

The world championships in 1999 were held at Melbourne; a more windy venue than the previous worlds in Dubai, and though that played more to Robert's strengths, it was one of the best performances I'd had up until then, and in really difficult conditions. It was a massive boost to win that event. Robert came second. It was odd, because before the regatta started I had been really struggling. I wasn't doing very well in training and, in the warm-up regatta, I finished very poorly. I remember speaking to my dad and he was trying to get me fired up. It must have worked as I was certainly on form by the time the world championships came around.

The Europeans in 1999 were also part of Olympic qualification for British sailors. It was important that I should finish in the top three, and I won quite comfortably. Then I had a difficult winter. I'd won the two world titles and that European. All seemed to be going well as I went down to New Zealand to prepare for the last world championships before the Olympics. They were due in March 2000, in Mexico. But I'd been on the go for quite a long time by then. I suffered a bit of a glitch. I was almost becoming stale. I think, if anything, I had been over-training. By this stage, I'd been training and racing all through the winter before, through the summer, and now into the winter again, without a real break.

It wasn't helped by a detour I made in my schedule. En route to Mexico from New Zealand, I'd agreed to compete in the Brazilian national championships, against Robert. That may sound a rather odd excursion. But I'd taken part in the event before, in January 1997. That was in Rio, and I'd actually won, and defeated Robert on his home waters, which felt good. I'd had a reasonably good experience, and it seemed like a sensible idea time-wise. I felt the stop-off would help with the jet lag between New Zealand and Mexico. As they say, it seemed like a good idea at the time . . .

The event was held in a place called Cabo Frio. It is a fishing and sailing town, with a population of around 120,000, a couple of hours south of Rio. I ended up staying in a pretty rough hotel which was right down the end of the river. The only way to get from the hotel back up to the town was in a little old rowing boat. As for sailing, I had chartered a boat. But it was a real dog; the slowest I'd ever been in a Laser in my life. Every race I'd come off the start line, and I'd be struggling for pace. Basically the whole fleet just ganged up on me. I'd tack and somebody else would tack on me. Then somebody else. I did two days of it, and then just packed my bags and left as quickly as I could. After the first day, Brazilian journalists were phoning me up and asking me why I wasn't sailing very well. It was a joke. As I've said, I was not feeling my usual self on the water anyway. This was not what I needed at all. It was definitely the right decision to just get out of there.

That said, I felt terrible leaving. It's not sporting to just up and quit. But something strange appeared to be going on. The only people enjoying my experience were the Brazilians, who were aware that I was the greatest threat to their man winning another Olympic gold. Whether I was right or wrong about that, I knew it was bad for my preparation.

In Mexico, at the worlds, I struggled again. The championships were important because if I finished in the top three, it meant I wouldn't have to take part in trials back in Britain for Olympic qualification. Though I was the number one in the GB rankings, I might not have won those trials.

Halfway through the event, Paul Goodison was third or fourth, and I was back in sixth or seventh, and I was struggling. I came good again, but even by the time we reached the final race I was still only fourth. Robert Scheidt was already world champion with one race to go. Michael Blackburn, the Australian, was second. Karl Sunesson, the Swede, was third. The year before Sunesson and I had competed in a regatta in France. He and I had been battling it out to finish first and second. In some events you end up with split fleets because there are so many boats. He had been watching a race that I was doing. There were very light, difficult conditions, and I was dead last. I remember going round a mark. Sunesson had been there in his boat, watching the race, and he had laughed at me.

I didn't say anything at the time, but it really riled me. I never forgot that.

At the 2000 world championships, this was my chance. It was quite a big ask. He was ten points in front of me going into the race. I needed to win the race, and beat him by ten places.

In fact, at the first windward mark things were not looking good. Sunesson was in the lead and I was lying in tenth, so, to say the least, I really had a lot on at this point. But I flew down the first run, downwind, overtook the ten boats, got the wind-shift, and now was just in front of him. But I still needed to win, and beat him by ten places. So, I set him up for an incident. We were both going along on a starboard tack, and at some stage he needed to tack to get to the mark, so he put himself down on a port tack which is the give-way tack.

As soon as he looked like he was about to tack, I bore away and was aiming straight for him. Karl hadn't looked before he tacked so he basically just tacked straight into me and fouled out. All he needed to do was do a penalty turn. We were a long way ahead of the rest of the fleet. For whatever reason he didn't take the penalty, leaving himself open to a protest. I won the race, and he was second. I protested him, and he was disqualified. I ended up third overall which was the overriding factor, where Sydney qualification was concerned. It felt good to put that one straight. Karl predictably didn't take it too well but he'd been asking for it and had pretty much dug his own grave by tacking where he did.

Paul Goodison had performed really well, finishing fifth overall. He agreed to come and train with me in Sydney, which was fantastic. Before that we did the final major pre-Olympic event, which was the European championships in Germany. Though we were training together, it all got a bit difficult because we were both close to winning the event. I ended up winning. Paul was second. But it was really tight in the last race. Paul had a really nice start, and got away from me. But our relative points tallies meant he needed to beat me by more than he did. It was close but he did not quite manage it, and though it became a rather stressful moment, we did well not to fall out with one another.

We went on down to Sydney, where we trained together for almost three months. As I explained earlier, Paul brought with him the crucial exprience of having grown up sailing on the lakes of the north of England. That made him a very talented sailor when there are tricky, light, changeable conditions. He gave me invaluable help that I needed in Sydney to improve in those circumstances. It was perfect preparation. I rented a house with Paul in Paddington which was near the sailing venue. My parents also came down and it was great to have that tight family support as the Olympics beckoned; the focus of my hopes and belief since standing on that podium at Savannah.

From one big event to the next over the intervening years, one of us, Robert Scheidt or I, had held sway. He won the 1997 world championships. The next year I triumphed, and then again in 1999. Though he won the immediate pre-Olympics world championships in 2000, as the Games approached, I sensed I was getting under his skin.

He was being pushed hard, and the tension was starting to mount.

Chapter 8

A Golden Day Followed by Death Threats

There was real anticipation in the air as the Sydney Olympic regatta began. Certainly, within myself – and, I suspect, from the public and the media. People appreciate sporting excellence; but more than that they love intense rivalry. Massive showdowns in any sport get the pulses quickening. That was the case here. Having won the 1998 and 1999 world championships, I sensed there was an expectancy that I would reverse my fortunes in Atlanta four years previously, and defeat Robert Scheidt.

Having been made BT Yachtsman of the Year and WS Atkins Inshore Yachtsman of the Year in January, I started the year in grand heart. One correspondent observed that those awards were 'a fitting reward for his 1999 domination of the Laser class across the world'. But he added the caveat: 'let's all hope he hasn't peaked too soon for the Sydney Olympics.' I was determined that there'd be no chance of that, even when Robert won the 2000 worlds, in which I finished third. After an indifferent start to that series I had finished well, and that was very pleasing as I prepared for Sydney.

At Atlanta I had started the regatta without any real pressure. Now, so much was expected of me. How would I handle the weight of expectancy?

I remember one journalist, writing afterwards about the situation, commented on how, compared to other sailors, I looked incredibly stressed throughout the whole event. But he then wrote that it was kind of understandable 'when you think that he was taking on one of the very best sailors in the world'. Which Robert was and still is. His record was there in stark black and white. He had won four world championships and an Olympics. He was seen as the guy who was going to be the best ever.

In truth, I wouldn't describe my own condition as stressed. I'd say it was more of an intense focus. The greater the challenge, the more focussed you have to be. This was my biggest test yet. To beat this guy, I knew I had to be one hundred per cent on my game.

Interviewers often ask me about stress and pressure in sport. Whether it's a golfer on the final tee of a major with a narrow lead, a footballer presented with a penalty shoot-out in a final, or in my case, outwitting the finest sailor in the world at the finale of an Olympics, none of us are totally immune from it. I like to think I'm better at dealing with it now because I'm older and less fazed by events, but I've always tried to become very detached. Single-mindedness takes over to the point that you have zero tolerance to any other considerations. You don't exactly become short with people, but that general leeway that you normally have to certain everyday things in life, you suddenly lose that as you focus on what matters. You ruthlessly put everything else aside. Little things, you just don't worry about.

The crucial thing in all sports is preparation. I genuinely felt I'd done mine as well, if not better, than most, in terms of time I'd spent, getting used to the conditions. My training partner Paul Goodison, who, subsequently, would go on to win a gold in Beijing, was invaluable in helping me acquit myself well in Sydney's uniquely difficult conditions.

It always had that potential to be a titanic battle. That's how it turned out, a final-day duel. Everything that had gone before, at Atlanta in 1996, and the world championships between then and now, had been close. It was just typical of our rivalry that it should come down to the two of us in the last race. The Australian representative, Michael Blackburn, was looking good for the bronze but neither Robert or I could do worse than silver.

Olympians will understand how I felt as I prepared for the finale on 29 September. If you miss out on a world title, there's another one next year. The Olympics are different. It does weigh on your mind. You never know how many opportunities you're going to get. You can't go back next year and right any wrongs. It's that factor which adds pressure to the whole thing.

Robert had a good first day. I had a better second and third day, and that continued through to the middle of the regatta. I established quite a good lead, but then Robert nailed the last couple of races before the final race. He hauled himself back into the lead by five points.

I remember the third from last race, where I'd been in a really good position. I was winning, but made a bad tactical error, and Robert overtook me and won. I finished fifth or sixth. I felt like the gold was slipping away from me after that race. I was really down. I said to my coach John: 'I can't let this guy beat me again.' I had worked so hard; I couldn't contemplate letting that happen. It meant so much.

We had two races on the last day. In the first, Robert got out into the lead and sailed a brilliant race. In contrast, I wasn't faring so well. I knew that to keep myself in with a chance of winning I had to finish in the top five. I was about seventh or eighth at the last mark. I had to get past three boats on the last run. To my relief, I just did that.

So, to the finale, which, for the uncommitted, promised to be a classic sporting encounter with the Brazilian. For my own supporters, it would be nerve-wracking. As I wrote at the start of this book, I had a dilemma in that final race. I could go out and attempt to beat Robert by ten places or more to win the gold. Or, because of the way discards worked (back then, you could discard your worst two races, now only one) and the fact that I'd had a much more consistent series than Robert, if I could knock him out of the race, he'd have to count one of his discarded races which was a big score, and that would give me the gold. The conditions were very fluctating and that also meant the vagaries of the elements could intervene.

People outside the sport don't understand how much conditions can affect a race. There is always an element of luck; but generally over eleven races that luck evens itself out. The best sailors win. You can't be lucky for eleven races. But if there's one race that counts, luck can come into play, and you can lose your medal. That was the case in Sydney. Conditions were completely random. It was a question of leaving it up to luck – or taking control of the situation. I opted unhesitatingly for the second option in conjunction with my coach John Derbyshire. It was important to me that I had John's endorsement of my tactics before that final race of the Laser series at Sydney. I knew what I had to do, and how I would approach it. But it's always good to have reassurance. As I mentioned earlier,

John's normally pretty conservative, a very straight guy. But when I described my plan to take Robert out, he responded immediately: 'If you're going to do that, make sure you do a proper job. If you're going to do that, you've got to really take him out.' Coming from him, that was quite funny. They turned out to be wise and prophetic words.

Most observers were enthralled by what took place. As Keith Wheatley of the *Sunday Times* wrote at the time:

> Not since 1983, when the cheeky Aussies and their winged keel grabbed the America's Cup from Dennis Conner, has a yacht race been as talked about as Ainslie's final bout. Absorbed spectators dissected the dodgem-car antics as the lanky kid from Lymington outmanoeuvred his deadly rival, Robert Scheidt.
>
> The Brazilian's critical error at the buoy when he suddenly gybed and crashed into Ainslie's oncoming dinghy was no simple misjudgement. Scheidt, 27, didn't become 1996 gold medallist and four-times world champion through mistaking a simple spin that a Sunday club sailor could pull off with ease.
>
> It was the desperate last throw of a man with nothing left to lose. Unable to get past the Briton on the water, Scheidt gambled that he might salvage something amid the claims and counterclaims of the protest room. Juries are notoriously fickle, and no different in sailing than at the Old Bailey.
>
> However, Ainslie's relaxed demeanour as he watched a video replay of the incident after the race showed how quietly confident he was. 'There's a bit of contact now and I think he's probably in the wrong,' murmured Big

Ben, with understated irony as the tape spooled. In the background, one or two team members chuckled. Unless all the jury members came from São Paulo it was obvious to anybody with a knowledge of sailing that Ainslie's case was watertight.

Throughout the interviews and the hearings, Scheidt was always 'he' or 'the Brazilian boat' when Ainslie spoke. Off the water, the two men are friends, have stayed in one another's homes and shared hotel rooms in their younger, impecunious days. On the water there is only a distant reserve, a staring tension. Much of it goes back to a July day four years ago in the final race of the Atlanta Olympics.

With Scheidt in gold-medal position and Ainslie breathing down his neck on silver, the far more experienced Brazilian knew that only the shy, slightly nervous boy next to him could take his title away. Slowly, and with infinite precision, glaring all the time into the younger man's boat, he pushed him towards the start line. With four seconds to go, and no time to turn back, the sharp white bow of Ainslie's Laser was across the line. A jury boat waved the black flag. Disqualification!

Disconsolate, and with the ever-present cap pulled down so low that nobody could see his face, Ainslie sailed back alone to the marina while Scheidt sailed off for the gold.

'What goes around, comes around,' he said yesterday, with a grin a mile wide. Scheidt avoided the medal-winner's press conference and stuck to his view that Ainslie had bent, if not broken, the rules.

Close friends say there had not been a day since Atlanta that Ainslie didn't think about that afternoon. Certainly he had never wavered by a millimetre in his determination to win the Laser gold medal at Sydney.

People make out that I just took the guy out of the race. But to stop one of the best sailors in the world finishing in the top twenty in a race is a huge ask. That's probably the biggest challenge you'll ever face in a yacht race. It's not as though I just ran into the guy and pulled him backwards. I had to do it within the rules, with pinpoint positioning, boat-handling, aggression, tactics, under that much pressure.

It never crossed my mind once that it was something I shouldn't have done, or it was unsporting. My job was to win a gold medal. I was representing the country. I had trained hard, and that's why you're there: to win. I have absolutely no qualms about what I did that day. I'd do the same again. In fact I did something similar at the Beijing Olympics. It is also something that happens with far more frequency now that the final race of the Olympics, the medal race, is not discardable and counts for double points, encouraging sailors to be more aggressive.

Other sailors' reactions were mixed. Some of Robert's supporters were a bit put out. There was some discussion after-wards about whether the rules, which, admittedly, are pretty complex in sailing, should be changed to stop such strategies. But most thought it was a fantastic piece of boat-handling and tactics. The general consensus was that this was the most exciting thing that had happened in dinghy sailing, possibly ever, but at least in the past ten years. Some of the older sailors I sail with, who weren't there, but are real legends of the sport, were intrigued. They just said: 'Tell us about Sydney. It sounds amazing.'

On the day, Robert didn't take it well at all. As I related at the start of my story, we came in off the water, and he put a two-part protest in. I put in a counter-protest. I said to him: 'Look, I can understand that, but you do realise that even if you win the protest, it won't make any difference to the overall result.' But Robert was adamant he was going to proceed, anyway. I eventually won my protest, and he got disqualified. Not that it made any difference to the overall result.

We had shaken hands, which pleased me, though it must have been hard for him. He disappeared quickly, as you'd expect, after the medal ceremony. He was devastated, as I'm sure I would have been in his situation. I left it for a couple of days. Then we were at one of the yacht clubs where there was a party going on. I tried to soften things. I went and bought him a drink from the bar and took it over. As I put the drink on the table, I said: 'For what it's worth, I think you're an amazing sailor. I've got a huge amount of respect for you.' He just said: 'Yeah, thanks,' or words to that effect. He didn't really want to know. I thought: 'Well, I've said my piece. I'll just leave it.' That was it. I didn't see him for another year or so.

The next time, he was fine – and our relationship has been good ever since. I doubt if we'll ever be best mates. We were fierce rivals, but that didn't mean I didn't have a huge amount of respect for him. I'd like to think that feeling was mutual. He's the toughest competitor I've ever raced against, and has given me the hardest racing I've ever had – and possibly will ever have.

The reaction from Brazil was not good. As I've already said, sailing is a major sport there. Guys like Robert are very popular and well known. It's a highly successful sailing nation, and people there are fanatical and take their success, or otherwise, very seriously. Some, apparently, too seriously. Already in 1996, after Robert and I had such a close race for the gold at those Games, I'd received a few cranky emails. To me they were clearly just meant as a joke but they were pretty offensive.

After the Sydney finale, I went down to the sailing centre the next day to be greeted by some police detectives. They were Australia's version of Special Branch, who dealt with security.

They sat me down, and said: 'Look, we don't want to worry you too much, but we've had these emails.'

I asked: 'What kind of emails?'

One said: 'They're kind of death threats.' Then he quickly added: 'But I wouldn't worry about it.'

They hadn't been sent to my own personal email address. At those Games, each athlete had an email account organised for them. Frankly, I hadn't even looked at mine. That's why I hadn't seen anything. But apparently, the security people had monitored everyone's, and intercepted these.

I was shown a few. They were abusive. Not very nice at all. I was told they'd tried to identify the senders, but that they could only trace them to a mail server based in Sydney. I was certain they had nothing to do directly with Robert. However, the policeman added: 'We don't think it's a real threat but we want to have someone watching you and we'll have some of our men at the medal ceremony.' I thought it was all a bit over the top. I didn't notice anyone following me but then these guys are pretty good at what they do.

To be honest, I was a little bit troubled by this. It was a bit full on. If I hadn't already experienced some of this in 1996 – and nothing had ever come of those – I'd have been more worried. Later, I heard there'd been effigies of me burnt on the streets of

São Paulo. I still don't know, to this day, if it's true or not. I suppose, if it was, you'd have to regard it as a compliment – of sorts! It was all a bit bizarre.

I then discovered that disgruntled observers weren't just based in South America. Sir Roger Bannister, the first four-minute miler, wrote quite a critical article, arguing that what I had done was not very sporting.

That really angered me at the time. I thought to myself: 'You may have been a great athlete, but you don't seem to understand the nature of this sport or the intricacies of sailing's rules.' Nor did he, and other critics, seem to appreciate how hard it is to pull off something like that.

Probably what irked me most of all was the fact that this happened in the Games which followed those of 1996. I felt like reminding Sir Roger, and others: remember Atlanta, when only Redgrave and Pinsent won a gold and everyone was complaining that our sportsmen and women were useless and didn't have a will-to-win attitude?

There had been all that criticism of our sportsmen not quite making it; not quite being good enough. Yet, here was someone who was prepared to go out and fight. Here was someone who'd gone out with a winning attitude, who's taken on the world's best in his sport, and won gold, and the response I got from Sir Roger was: 'Tut, tut, it's not sporting.' It infuriated me at the time. But in the context of my entire career, as I remarked previously, there was no point dwelling on it. I just had to move on. I did meet Sir Roger once, but I never mentioned it. What would have been the point? Let's just say now that I found it very disappointing.

Other articles also questioned whether my tactics had been fair, but people in sailing were resoundingly clear that I had been in the right. It was covered by the rules. It had happened before in sailing, though not really at the Olympics. Most pertinently of all, the way the sport has gone since, and the way Olympic sailing has developed, the medal race was introduced. That actively tries to encourage such scenarios, where someone will attempt to sail down an opponent to ensure that they win the gold, and adds to the excitement. In a way, what I did was ahead of its time. Something similar happened in four or five of the medal races in Beijing. I repeated that tactic with the American in my class. I just needed to make sure I beat him, or sailed him down the fleet. That's the way the sport's gone. Sir Roger, and anyone else who had any argument with what I did at Sydney, has been proved wrong.

Despite certain aspects of the aftermath, it's probably the most enjoyable Games I've ever done, in terms of the venue, the city, the Australian people, the weather and culture. Looking forwards to the London Olympics I hope that people in the UK and especially Londoners embrace the Games and can create a similar carnival-like atmosphere as, to me, this is what will make the difference between a good Games and a great Games.

What was so attractive about Sydney as a venue was the fact that, for the first time, sailing was in the centre of the Games. Being staged in the harbour was brilliant. Winning helped, too, of course. And I wasn't the only British victor. Shirley Robertson won gold in the Europe class. I was so pleased for her because she had so narrowly missed out on a medal in Atlanta, finishing fourth. My great friend Iain Percy won gold in the Finn. Ian Walker, who had been crewing for John Merricks when they won silver in the 470 in Atlanta, had teamed up with Mark Covell to contest the Star class. They won silver, as did

Simon Hiscocks and Ian Barker in the 49er class. It was a magnificent team effort.

I'm not a great one for 'what ifs?'. But I sometimes look back and wonder what life would have been like if I'd won that gold first time, at the Atlanta Games. I suspect it would have been very different. By the time Beijing came around, I could have been challenging oarsman Matthew Pinsent's record of four golds in Beijing, with the possibility of equalling Steve Redgrave's at London 2012. But I would also have been rushed into the limelight far more quickly than I have been. In a way, winning the silver first time was quite a good thing for me. Such close proximity to success made me even more determined to train that much harder to try and win a gold next time.

Chapter 9

Up for the Cup

The Olympic challenge is hard to beat. It's about getting, more or less, straight out on to the water, and raw sailing, on your own. In the single-handed discipline, at least, you take the glory; you accept the blame.

Yet, as you get older, you begin to look for those new challenges, in terms of management and business and team-building. The contrast with Olympic sailing can hardly be more extreme when you first venture into the world of the America's Cup – a phenomenon that the American TV mogul Ted Turner, and skipper of the 1977 winner *Courageous*, once described as 'a battlefield of wits, muscle and money'.

So much goes into just getting an America's Cup boat from the dock to the water. It can take about four hours, and involves smooth organisation and highly efficient teamwork. The difference between that and Olympic sailing could hardly be more pronounced. And not just because of the potential rewards.

You don't have to be a sailing aficionado to know that the America's Cup exudes glamour. There are many parallels with Formula 1, including the fact that many millions are expended on design and technical expertise and on employing the world's finest sailors. The financial rewards for success in the Cup can be substantial and the event can yield a great economic boost to the host city's economy.

America's Cup competition has produced some formidable characters and, not surprisingly, on occasions, a collision of egos. Russell Coutts and Brad Butterworth are the most successful Cup sailors there have ever been. Together they spearheaded the New Zealand victories in 1995 and 2000 and then went on to win the 2003 Cup for the Swiss billionaire Ernesto Bertarelli and his Alinghi team.

Being involved with a successful British America's Cup team had been a dream for me ever since that time, growing up in Cornwall, when *Victory 83* and its sister yacht, owned by the entrepreneur Peter de Savary, the owner of Falmouth Docks, had sailed around the harbour. I still recalled from time to time that occasion when I had gone out with a mate of mine in his father's speedboat, and watched them and how I'd imagined myself being on board. I was only about 12 at the time. Now, ten years later, I was to get my chance.

I had read all the books about an event which had first been staged in 1851 when a schooner, named *America*, commissioned by the New York Yacht Club, overcame a fifteen-strong British fleet in a race around the Isle of Wight. The British accused the Americans of taking a shorter course, and there were even suggestions that they'd boosted their yacht's speed with the employment of a steam-driven propeller. Ultimately, though, the US were declared the victors.

They had continued that domination until 1983 when Alan Bond's *Australia II*, skippered by John Bertrand, defeated Dennis Conner's *Liberty*. I was familiar with names like Bond, Ted Turner, Sir Peter Blake and, of course, Russell Coutts. But I didn't actually know a lot about the demands of skippering a Cup yacht, as I hoped one day to do.

As I prepared for Sydney in 2000, it looked as though a really exciting opportunity had been offered to me once the Games were over. For me, it meant a transition from single-handed demands, where my fate was solely in my own hands, to the team ethic.

When I first became involved, I wasn't a dreamer. I was aware that money, ambition and egos can be potentially explosive chemicals when placed in the pestle and mortar of elite multi-crewed sailing. Yet, what began with anticipation turned into one of the most disappointing and frustrating episodes of my career as I walked away from one of the top teams. It was quite possibly the worst experience of my life.

But to return to the beginning of that episode. I was out training in Sydney six months before the 2000 Games when I received an email, out of the blue, from an Australian named Peter Gilmour. It was something of a shock. I had met him before at a match-racing regatta when I was crewing for Chris Law – then the top match-racer in the UK – doing the tactics in the Australia Cup. We actually won it, and Peter was also there with his team, so presumably he remembered me.

I was well aware that Peter was very well respected in the sport, a very successful America's Cup skipper who had sailed in five Cups, three as skipper. In 2000, he had skippered the Japanese team. He'd won match-racing world championships a number of times and had a reputation of being one of the top America's Cup sailors around.

I'd already heard, through the sailing press, that one of the new teams for the 2003 Cup was a set-up called OneWorld. It looked like being some team. It was co-owned by the Seattle-based Craig McCaw, a telecommunications billionaire and at the time one of the wealthiest men in the US. This was supposed to be the 'dream team', with Gilmour as skipper and the designer Laurie Davidson, who had been responsible for the two previous New Zealand America's Cup-winning boats. There was also a whole host of the Kiwi crew, who'd been enticed across for big money to sail with this new team. This, I should add, was at the time of the exodus of Russell Coutts and Brad Butterworth from Team New Zealand to Alinghi, the Swiss team. Many leading American sailors were also in the crew.

If there was ever a time to get involved with the America's Cup, this seemed like the ideal opportunity. It was just a fantastic team: many of the top sailors from the last winning team, the designer of the boat, all the money in the world you could ask for. Yes, you could say I was interested!

I kept in touch with Peter, and then two months before the Games we met up in Australia. He has a house, thirty miles north of Sydney, in Paradise Waters on the shores of Pittwater, a beautiful place. I drove over to see him. We chatted, he told me about his ideas for the team, and we shook hands.

There was one crucial omission in our discussions. They included no specific role for me. In one sense, that was logical. Where Peter was concerned, I was just a young talented guy who'd had no experience of the America's Cup. I'd hardly done any big-boat sailing. In hindsight, I should have been more circumspect. I should never have left things so open-ended. The reality was that, from single-handed sailing, I would be just one of a group of seventy people in someone else's team. But I suppose Peter talked it up a little bit. He suggested it would be good for me to try all the positions on the boat, see what worked best. He was very positive about the whole thing.

At the time, Peter publicly explained my inclusion thus: 'There's no question Ben is a junior guy here in terms of America's Cup experience. There are so many winners in this team that even *I* feel privileged to be part of it. It's like having cogs of different sizes. It's a question of finding which ones mesh together the best, and Ben is one of the key cogs. We targeted Ben for what he is: one of the proven winners in sailing.'

I talked it all through with my father and, more than anything, we saw it as a great opportunity; working and sailing with that calibre of sailor. I jumped at it. In hindsight, I didn't think enough about what it meant in terms of lifestyle, at that age. I was on my own. And this would be a long haul of several months. Probably in retrospect, at 22, 23, I was too young to get involved in a project like that. I made some great friends in the team but I was going in on my own, with little support.

Anyway, I agreed a deal, but I didn't sign anything immediately. Then I got my head back into preparation for the Games.

After Sydney, another tantalising America's Cup possibility appeared on the horizon. Peter Harrison announced that he was going to put together a GB team. The then 65-year-old, a computer entrepreneur and sailing enthusiast, who'd won a number of trophies down the years, planned an America's Cup challenge – the first involvement of this nation in fifteen years.

Of course, that was of great interest, too. Initially, there were a few candidates who could have been considered for the team and to lead it. I attended the original meeting with Iain Percy, who'd just won a gold in the Finn at Sydney, together with Ian

Walker, who'd won silver in the 470 at the Atlanta Games and in the Star at Sydney, and Chris Law.

Chris was then quite a bit older than the rest of us, at mid to late 40s. Earlier in his career, he'd won a Finn Gold Cup, aged 23, in 1976, and represented GB in the 1984 Olympics, in the Soling class, finishing in fourth place, and had also been helmsman in the last British challenge, *White Crusader*, back in 1987. Sadly, he passed away, aged only 55, in 2008. I crewed for Chris in three match-racing regattas during 1996 and 1997, two of which we won and in the other we were last. I guess that was Chris. When he was on fire, he was undoubtedly one of the best sailors in the world. The trick was getting the best out of his complex character but I am grateful I had the chance to sail with him.

Anyway, the four of us met, and talked about a way to go forward. We agreed that Ian Walker would go and meet Peter Harrison to discuss plans further. When he returned, we heard that Ian was in charge, and running everything. The rest of us may be hired to do specific roles, but there were no guarantees. For some reason it just didn't feel right. I wasn't sure if the team was being set up with enough experience to be successful.

Everything suggested that I should take the OneWorld option. What really swayed me, though, was going off on holiday to the Virgin Islands with my then girlfriend Boel on a charter boat. We were sailing to a place called Bitter End, one of the top resorts there. We found ourselves in the middle of loads of yachts. It was obvious there was a race going on. We happened to sail behind one boat, and I noticed a guy at the helm with a highly distinctive, wide moustache, reminding me of Captain Hook! I said to Boel: 'That looks just like Paul Cayard,' the best-known American sailor since his compatriot, the great America's Cup skipper, Dennis Conner. Then we passed another boat, and I said 'That looks just like Russell Coutts.' It was, and it turned out that these sailors were taking part in a pro-am regatta.

We sailed into the harbour, and discovered all these famous America's Cup sailors. We stopped off and had a drink with the guys. I remember talking to Paul Cayard, who had started his America's Cup career when he was about 19, and had been competing for thirty, forty years. The most important thing I gleaned from him was that in the America's Cup you have to be in a competitive team. It's hard work, a tough event, and if you're not successful it's probably the worst thing you can undertake in your sailing career. That discussion confirmed my intuition that I should go for the OneWorld challenge. For me, the GB project was not going to be successful because it didn't have the design firepower and the team was relatively inexperienced. In contrast, I had this offer to go with the top team, with its successful designers, and which was really well funded. There was no doubt which route I should follow.

I was very happy to sign up for a leading crew, although I knew it would be vastly different to the sailing with which I was familiar. To repeat, I had absolutely no experience of America's Cup sailing at all, and it was important for me to start learning what that involved. I was certain I could make the transformation from a single-handed sailor, and that I could readily become part of a team. There are many positive aspects I took from being involved with OneWorld, and later Team New Zealand; both were very good teams and – with the exception of the one area that I'll come to – well run. They were good people. There was no messing around with poor management. I could see how a top-level team functioned.

This was also the first time I had a solid income. As I've said already, from when I was a child, I've always been a worrier, and particularly about money. Like anyone else, I've always thought: 'How am I going to make a living?' I don't come from a particularly wealthy background. No family trusts, or anything like that!

Considering back then there was no money in Olympic sailing, I was fortunate that for the 2000 Games I had a sponsor, Colonial, the Australian financial services group. That helped cover the costs. Then suddenly, at age 22, here I was, being offered, well, not quite the same as a top footballer but a lot of money . . . and a three-year contract.

A few people in America's Cup sailing are highly rewarded. Those who approach the level of, say, a Russell Coutts, would have earned a fortune. That's not a great secret. It's a little like a top European football league. If someone wants to come along and establish a dream team, it's going to cost them an awful lot of money to get top guys in the world to sail for them. When you, as a skipper or another member of the afterguard – the 'brains' of the boat – can talk to a number of teams, that places you, just like a footballer, in a very advantageous negotiating position. Even other members of the crew can be well rewarded.

That said, when I started out, I had the philosophy that I would never sail for money. I always tried to remain faithful to that core value. I would always do what was right for my sailing, and what I wanted to achieve. I've actually been lucky so far. There's never been any conflict. I've never had to decide between one course being better for my sailing career and another paying me more money.

There are a lot of professional sailors who just do whatever is the highest-paying job. This is not a criticism, but I find that quite sad, in a way. They're obviously not as motivated as they would be if they were doing it for the love of it. I don't think you get the best out of people that way. It's no different from other sports, particularly football, where some players are trying to milk the system for as much as they can get. The really good ones just focus on being with the best team they can, so have a chance of winning a Champions League, Premier League, whatever. And that's what I believed I had done here by joining up with OneWorld.

It wasn't long, however, before I began to realise that the America's Cup can have its downsides, particularly for a rookie . . .

First of all there was moving home. Back then, the America's Cup had a residency rule. If you weren't a national of the team you were with, you had to be a resident. All the non-US nationals had to become US 'residents'. That meant staying there for all the time we weren't sailing in New Zealand or Europe. OneWorld's base was Seattle Yacht Club. So, Seattle became our 'home'.

After the Olympics, we started preparing for the America's Cup that November in Auckland. We did two or three months sailing, and then moved to Seattle, where we lived for about four months. Now the Pacific North-West is an incredibly beautiful place. Absolutely gorgeous. Except you can't sail there. Not seriously. There's no wind, and it just rains all the time! Or seems to. All we did was have numerous team meetings, lots of gym training, and, well, lots of skiing. We used to escape to the spectacular resort of Whistler – location, incidentally, of the 2010 Winter Olympics – in British Columbia which was only about two and half hours' drive away. So, though it wasn't a hardship, we didn't actually do a lot of sailing.

Our sailing was confined to the European summer, doing the European circuit in 2001, and we then went back down to New Zealand for their summer at the end of the year, and trained in the America's Cup boats. OneWorld had bought a couple of them from a previous America's Cup team.

What were my initial impressions of America's Cup boats? My first sight of the OneWorld set-up took me aback. As I told sailing journalist Tim Jeffery when he wrote about this new venture for me at the time: 'Walking through the gates and seeing the size of the compound and everything that goes into launching the boats, and keeping them running, is just incredible. The resources, the details, and sheer breadth of what is covered is impressive. The first couple of weeks has been a big learning experience.' On the water, too, it was pretty over-whelming. The first time you go out, your initial impression is how noisy they are. There are creaking noises from the loads involved. It sounds as though the boat's breaking up the whole time.

After my early career where I spent so much time travelling, either driving across Europe to events with a 14ft Laser on my roof, or months at a time spent training in the US, Australia or New Zealand, here I was confronted by the spectacle of boats 75ft long, with the keel alone weighing around twenty tons, and carrying a crew of seventeen. As Tim Jeffery described my move at the time: 'In one step, Ainslie has gone from being a solitary go-kart driver into the McLaren Formula 1 team, such is the difference between campaigning with the Laser and being a Cup sailor.'

However, my anticipation was tempered by the fact that, from my first introduction to the team, there existed an over-whelming concern: where would I fit in?

Peter Gilmour is a hugely talented sailor, an exceptionally nice guy and a consummate professional. The problem was that he was the skipper *and* team principal, so Peter also ended up doing most of the running of the campaign. That meant his time was stretched, and he was probably not as focussed as he could have been.

That made it tough for me. With no defined role, as such, the general idea was that I would try a few things and see how I fit in. There always tends to be a little political infighting, and I had expected that, but immediately I sensed this perception of me being the young buck, having come out of Sydney with a gold medal looking to make my name in the America's Cup arena. I guess a few guys probably had their antennae up. I remember one very well known American sailor telling me that winning a gold medal 'meant Jack Shit in the America's Cup'. I raised my eyebrows and got on with loading sails.

Initially, they had me doing different jobs. I was happy with that because I was learning. But I hoped that, at some stage, I might get the chance to do some helming. The first thing I did, for the first month, was the runners, the backstays, which hold the mast up. It's one of those jobs that you can never do well, but if you do it badly the mast will fall down. So, it's a major responsibility!

I managed to ease the runners so quickly because I didn't really do it properly, and it flicked all the windgear off the top of the mast. So, I got taken off the runners and got the job of the guy who has to go up the mast to look for the best wind on the course and to help with sail-handling in manoeuvres. That was exhilarating, in one way, but also probably the scariest moment.

'Just keep looking up, and you'll be fine,' I was assured by 'Smithy', Alan Smith, one of the very best bowmen in the business. They hoisted me up the mast, which was ninety-odd feet. To give an idea of that, think of roughly three times the height of a typical house. I just kept looking up. I've got a reasonable head for heights, but I got to the top, looked down, and thought 'f★★★★★ hell'. From the sea, you couldn't normally see Auckland itself. It was obscured by North Head. But now from the top of the mast you could see over North Head, back to the city. It was pretty freaky. Smithy shouted up to check I was OK and I think I whimpered something about being fine but, in reality, I was absolutely shitting myself.

It's not as though your view is from a stable, fixed point. Those America's Cup masts are pretty flexible, and move around a lot in the wind. As you can imagine, it took a while for me to get into that responsibility . . .

Tim Jeffery wrote in an article at the time: 'Having a gold medal round his neck brings no rights or privileges. It just marks the young Briton out for good-natured needling. The New Zealand winch grinders, Andy "Raw Meat" Taylor and Craig Monk, are sweet-natured men who love to prove that no T-shirt on earth is big enough or strong enough for their massive torsos. "Yeah, we got a Pommie gold medallist pumping the bilges out before we go yachting," growled "Meat", with a beatific grin on his face. Ainslie, after two weeks with the team, has not quite got the killer retort yet, but it will come. As the new boy, he has been put on the grinders, sent 100ft up the rig and given the boat to steer – a crash course in the carbon-fibre Cup-class yachts.'

After that, I started operating as tactician to Peter Gilmour. We did a few match-racing regattas. The first one, the Australia Cup, we won. So, that was a really good start. We seemed to have a good relationship going. It looked promising when I then started doing tactics for Peter in the Cup boats. But with the bigger boats it's a whole different game, of thinking ahead more, knowing the manoeuvres. I didn't know any of that. I hadn't done it before. I needed more time to get into that role. Because of the team being the way it was, and the type of people involved, there were quite high expectations.

In truth, I think, with the team progressing, the decision was that they didn't want to invest time in bringing me up to be the tactician or helmsman because they already had really good people anyway. I had to face it. After about six months, it became obvious that there wasn't really a position for me in the team. I was just going round, trying lots of different roles. It was good learning, but I was never actually going to end up with a significant job.

There came a breaking point. I must stress here that there were a lot of really good guys on that team who helped me a lot. I had made some good mates, with guys like Kelvin Harrap, Ben Durham and James Spithill, the very talented Australian who went on to helm the OneWorld boat in the Cup. However not everyone was as supportive. When things got tough, I had no one to back me up. No one to fight my corner.

For two or three months, I had struggled with the situation, and all the time was thinking about what to do. I was still only in my early 20s. I had to make the decision: should I stay or go? It all came to a head one day as we were doing a practice race. My job was to go and help pull the jib (a sail set in front of the mast) down after the spinnaker (a large downwind sail, set from a spinnaker pole) had been hoisted. It meant going from the back of the boat to the front. It was a really tight situation, and one of the guys at the back was out of place. We were doing a gybe, and there was no one to pull the new runner on. I stayed behind to do that; otherwise, basically, the mast was going to fall down.

Once I'd done that, and went forwards to help with the jib, one of these super-experienced guys, who otherwise I got on with fine, really laid into me and started giving me a whole load of grief because I wasn't there to pull the jib down. I thought to myself: 'Mate, are you so stupid that if I hadn't actually stayed behind to pull the runner on we wouldn't even be sailing because the mast would have fallen down.' My next thought was: 'I can't take this any more. This is just doing my head in.'

It was the toughest decision I've ever had to make. At the time, I wondered if I'd blown any future chances I'd have of being involved in the America's Cup. No one likes to walk out on a team, and certainly not one containing fifty per cent of the personnel who'd just won the last Cup. Least of all me, a newcomer to it. You'll inevitably be perceived as unreliable, and that's not great for your reputation. But at the same time, I was just hating it so much. I felt that I just had to get back to Olympic sailing.

I made up my mind. I decided it wasn't working, and I ended up walking out. It was a really tough decision to make. That was a big move. A really tough call. I had to have a huge amount of confidence that I could go back to Olympic sailing, resume my career, and win another medal. It pretty much could have meant my sailing career was over.

Coincidentally, before that, representatives of the British challenge had got back in touch. They were looking for another helmsman. That would have been one way out – except I'd signed a non-compete clause in my contract. I started talking to Peter Gilmour about the possibility of pulling out of my contract so that I could join the GB challenge. He said: 'Well, they could maybe do that – if they pay us a transfer fee,' as in football. He came up with a ridiculous amount, $1 million I think it was, that they'd have to pay to get me out of the contract.

The upshot of it all was that I returned to Olympic sailing. However, despite my insistence that all I wanted to do was to return home and buy a Finn dinghy – the class I had decided to move into from the Laser – and get back into single-handed sailing, I still had a feeling that Peter Gilmore was a little paranoid and I would try and break my contract.

It didn't end there. Worse was to follow. The day I departed, Peter suggested I should go along to the team base and explain myself to the whole team as to why I was leaving. It was quite possibly the worst thing I've ever had to do. You've got all these guys assembled, many of whom had won the America's Cup. It was pretty tough. All I could say was: 'Look, I've learnt so much, and it may seem ridiculous to be walking away from such a great team. When I arrived here, I couldn't even wind a winch. I probably still can't.'

I have to admit it was a rare moment in my career when I got massively down. I was actually going out on the water and absolutely hating every minute of it. That was anathema to me. For a sport you are supposed to love, it is not a great position to dread setting foot on a boat. I wanted to make it work. When things got really bad, I didn't want to be regarded as a quitter. But it became obvious that it was just a waste of time.

I spoke to my dad, who could tell how distressed I was with the whole thing. He said: 'It doesn't matter what it is – it's no good for you if it's making you upset.'

He was great, and very supportive. He helped me to deal with it. I felt embarrassed, in a way, because I'd left such a great team. I hadn't done the America's Cup before; hadn't realised the way it all worked, and should have got more confirmation from Peter Gilmour about what my role would be in the team. I agree. That was my mistake.

But I didn't make excuses, or blame anyone else. I've always tried to be candid about my performances. If I haven't sailed well, I will admit that – at least to myself. If you're honest to yourself about your faults, that's when you start improving the most. What happed in my introduction to America's Cup sailing was really disappointing, but, in a way, it just motivated me to be more successful in the Finn.

OneWorld proceeded to finish third in the Louis Vuitton Cup. The winner of that series is the challenger which goes forward to contest the America's Cup against the defending syndicate. That was Alinghi. In the 2003 America's Cup, held in Auckland, the Swiss boat, skippered by Russell Coutts, vanquished Team New Zealand, skippered by Dean Barker.

The British challenge, whose personnel eventually included skipper Ian Walker and tactician Adrian Stead, a member of the Olympic team of 1996, went out in the quarter-finals of the Louis Vuitton Cup. The British team showed some early promise but got distracted by designing and building a radical second yacht with little time to maximise its potential.

As for myself, well, it turned out to be probably the best decision I've ever made – though, at the time, that's not exactly the way I viewed matters.

The way things transpired was actually a godsend. It gave me the freedom to go and sail the Finn, which I loved doing – and still enjoy sailing today, which may not have been the case had I stayed with OneWorld and become increasingly frustrated. What had happened gave me two and a half years to prepare for the next Olympics in a new class of boat. Only six months later,

I would win the world and European Finn championships. That was a massive relief, and an important step.

If I'd have persevered and gone through with it and competed in the 2003 America's Cup, it would have made it very difficult, in such a short period of time, to make the change to the Finn sufficiently to do myself justice in Athens.

When I had won that Olympic silver at Atlanta it had been a rewarding moment, but I felt I'd never get another chance to win a gold. Now that seems ridiculous, but it summed up my approach at that time. Back then, I was in a rush to do everything. I know now that I had been in too much haste to get involved with the America's Cup.

Yet, despite everything I have said, there were also positives from that experience: I had spent a year learning what the America's Cup was all about, got paid well, and benefited from a lot of insight into how a good team – because it was that – is structured and managed. Though I had a lot to learn, I had gained a good overview of how to sail Cup boats, and went through most of the positions. I had a good feeling for what it was about. And I wanted to return to it one day. I was fortunate enough to be offered the chance. But first the prospect of Athens demanded all my attention.

Chapter 10

Fired by Adversity to Athens Gold

The Laser had been good for me, but as I looked ahead to Athens I decided to make the transition to the more technically complex and demanding Finn class.

Both are single-handed classes, with one sail and similar hull shapes. But the Finn is a much heavier boat, and it takes a heavier guy to sail it. You need to be around 90–100kg, while to sail the Laser the weight range is about 76–81kg. Wherever you go in the world, the Laser is exactly the same. The Finn can have variations in design, within very tight tolerances. You can design different hulls, foils and rigs. In other words, you can change the set-up of the boat which you can't with the Laser. It brings a whole new technical aspect to racing.

I thought that was important. I thought it was a change I needed to make at this stage in my career to be successful in the sport. My good fortune, when I made the transition, was having David Howlett, nicknamed 'Sid', who had coached Iain Percy to gold in 2000 in the Finn, to prepare me. He was also known as the 'medal-maker' because of his prowess as a coach.

For me, Howlett, a former Olympic Finn sailor himself, was the guru when it came to the technical nuances of the Finn dinghy. He was always open to new ideas – even from completely different sports. A huge Gunners fan, he paid a visit, with Royal Yachting Association chief executive Rod Carr, to Arsenal's then new training facility, and spoke with Arsène Wenger about what both sports could learn from each other.

Sid was so fanatical about Arsenal that, at one of the sports awards, he insisted that I get him Patrick Vieira's autograph. Sheepishly I went up to the Arsenal midfielder and captain, shoving pen and paper in front of him with the old excuse, actually true on this occasion, that I wanted the autograph for someone else. He dropped the pen and as we both bent down for it we managed to headbutt each other. I thought it was quite amusing and laughed that he got far worse abuse from Roy Keane. I don't think he got the joke and went off rubbing his head.

I arrived back from New Zealand and the America's Cup adventure in January 2002, and got straight into the new boat. I went round to Sid's house. He talked me through the Finn and what it was about, and we then went down to his local sailing club in Warsash, near Southampton, where there was an old boat of Iain Percy's floating around. We spent a couple of days going through how to set the boat up, and what was important. Then I got into this craft, and just started sailing around on my own for a couple of weeks.

Meantime Sid helped me get hold of a good second-hand boat, and a decent, soft rig, because I was still quite light for the boat. We arranged to have it sent down to Palma where there was a training camp ahead of the first big regatta of the year. I did a week's training, then the regatta. All the top Finn sailors were there. But after the first two days of the event I was in the lead. I never looked back.

Admittedly, as I've mentioned, I still had quite a light frame and the relatively light winds helped me. But I knew then that I'd done the right thing to leave OneWorld. That whole episode had been a really serious knock to my confidence. I had felt like a complete failure. It felt so good to be back racing and doing well; a huge relief and confidence boost.

People say I always appear confident in my ability, maybe there's even a touch of arrogance. But you always worry. There have been times, and this was one, when you need to go out and prove to yourself that you can still do it.

Some Finn sailors take years to get to the top. So, how did I reach the required standard so quickly? Well, Sid saved me a year or so, messing around, trying to get the right settings. I just set the boat using his advice and my own feel. Now, looking back, I know it was actually set up slightly wrong, but I didn't worry about that. Most of the other sailors were more worried about getting their boats absolutely spot on. I was confident that I had the boat set up near enough. I just went out and raced with the kit I had, and started winning. Later on, when I got more confidence in the boat, and my own feel for it, I started adjusting settings more to how I felt, and then made another jump in boat speed. Millimetres here and there can make a big difference.

The first couple of years were odd in a way. I won world and European championships in each of my first two years, 2002 and 2003, even though I probably didn't have the boat set up that well, and wasn't actually that quick. I just sailed really well. In my third year, which was the Games year, I acquired a new boat and tried a new rig, a different set-up, and got the boat going a lot quicker. That was quite crucial when it came to the Athens Games in 2004.

Meanwhile I had been building up my physique. Not that I would ever have pretensions of joining the musclemen of body-building. However, it did involve a lot of gym time and a huge change in diet. I had always had to keep my weight down for the Laser and now I was into three protein shakes a day and basically doubling my portions. It's not everyone's ideal routine, but I really enjoyed the challenge of getting down the gym and lifting heavy weights.

My progress could not have been better, until I suffered a serious complication. I got really sick in the winter of 2003-4 while training in Spain for the world championships in Rio in January. I became really depressed and moody and had no energy. I didn't know what was wrong with me. That was really tough; trying to push myself through this really heavy fitness programme, while feeling very low from a very debilitating condition. I somehow battled my way through the world championships, and managed to win them.

I had to come back to the UK to see a doctor. My condition was diagnosed as glandular fever. I've never really got over it one hundred per cent. I still suffer from its effects occasionally. At the time, it meant that I couldn't do any training at all for about ten weeks. In an Olympic year, that's far from ideal. But that's been my fate since then. My preparations for, and start of Olympic Games have never been simple. There's always something goes wrong.

But you have to deal with such setbacks.

While my Laser rival Robert Scheidt was, no doubt, pleased to see me depart on a new adventure, my new rivals saw me as a serious threat. In my first year in the Finn, there had been what

I'd describe as a bit of gang warfare. They were all very friendly off the water, but I definitely got the feeling that a few of the sailors were trying to intimidate me, and make life as difficult as they could on it. I managed to come through that. But in my first European championships I was involved in something like five protests. Crazy. It was similar in the world championships, but I managed to prevail and win both events. I had shattered the established order early on. That made a pretty big statement to all concerned.

I qualified for Athens through the world championships at Cadiz, in 2003. They also served as GB selection trials. That was a tough one, because one of my very best friends, Bart Simpson, was also competing for Olympic qualification. Bart is also very close to Iain Percy and had trained with him in Sydney before the 2000 Games. It was thought he would take Iain's place in the Finn, but Bart was struggling with his kit and having problems with his equipment. Then I came into the class, and enjoyed great success straight away. It's difficult when it's one of your best mates that you're trying to compete against and beat.

Bart and I had started off travelling together for the first year. We went everywhere together. But it placed too much of a strain on the friendship. It chips away at it. We eventually started travelling separately instead. That was the right thing to do. It took the pressure off.

In the worlds, Bart sailed really well. He got his kit sorted out and sailed one of his best events. He finished third, but I just won after an incredibly tight final race. That was hard for him to take, but he was great about it, and came back to win that amazing gold with Iain in the double-handed Star class at Beijing.

In the build-up to Athens, training had gone very encouragingly at the venue. It had been a fantastic preparation in the new boat. The tuning had gone well. I had been greatly helped by Charlie Cumbley, Matt Howard and Chris Brittle who'd come down and trained with me, together with Bart. Some foreign rivals would also come and try and train with us. Sid was keen that we shouldn't impart information to the 'enemy'. He liked to use the old wartime slogan 'Loose Lips Sink Ships'. However, we'd maybe do one session with them but always had the option to do our own thing and our own testing. You could see that bothered the opposition, which was a great fillip for me, psychologically.

The week before the Games, I decided to taper down the training. Frankly, for whatever reason, it wasn't going very well. I was struggling a bit. I'd definitely got a case of what I'd have to describe as nerves. I was really apprehensive. I thought 'Shit, what's going on?' I wondered if I'd trained too much. All these doubts came into my mind. I just had to use my experience to get through it. You always know that occasionally you'll have bad days. You just have to keep doing the same things, and not panic.

As I've said, there was no Robert Scheidt this time. The Laser was his forte. We were probably both relieved to see the back of each other! In the Finn, the biggest danger was the Pole, Mateusz Kusznierewicz, who had won gold in the class at Atlanta and finished fourth in Sydney; the Spaniard, Rafael Trujillo; and the Belgian Sébastien Godefroid.

After the Olympics opening ceremony, the then prime minister, Tony Blair, and his wife Cherie came along to the sailing venue at Agios Kosmas to wish us well. I had a chat with Tony for a while. He said: 'I've heard about you. I've heard you're really aggressive on the water, but a really nice guy on land.'

I told him that there are two sides to a lot of sportsmen. And added: 'A bit like politicians . . .' He was a likeable-enough guy and you could see why he had such an appeal as he had that great ability to relate to pretty much anyone. Cherie was quite full on but also very pleasant and we were very grateful that they had taken the time to wish us luck.

Though I suppose it was good PR for them, I appreciated the gesture. It was something of a distraction, but, in a way, was probably a good thing. After that, we got refocussed and started racing.

My first day on the water was a complete fiasco. I had a really bad first race, and finished twelfth. In the second race, the breeze was a bit steadier, and, by that stage, I knew which side of the course was going to be favoured. I got a reasonable start and had a really good contest with the Pole, Kusznierewicz, in which we both overtook each other. He ended up winning, and I was second. I was a little disappointed, but at least it was a great improvement on the first race. Kusznierewicz had a first and second that day, so it was looking good for him.

I sailed back to the harbour, checked my boat, packed it up and headed to the accommodation, looking forward to a good meal cooked up by the excellent team chef Mel Gray. I had just got out of the shower to hear my mobile was ringing. I answered the phone and very quickly got a sinking feeling in my stomach. It was Chris Gowers, Paul Goodison's coach, who had checked the protest board and at the very last possible moment my old adversary from France, Guillaume Florent, had put in a protest against me. I straight away knew what this was about. I had done nothing wrong, but I also knew that I was suddenly in very deep water.

Sailing rules are complex, but I should explain at this stage the kind of offence that can get you into trouble.

The sailor with wind on his left-hand side is on port tack. If he has wind on his right-hand side he is on starboard tack. The boat with wind coming from his right-hand side, i.e. on starboard tack, has the right of way if he is on a collision course with another competitor. It is the responsibility of the other sailor to keep clear, or tack, or change course to keep out of the other boat's way.

A similar problem occurs when boats are travelling in either a windward or leeward direction. The windward boat is moving towards the wind; the leeward boat away from the wind. If these two boats are on a collision course, or overlap, the windward boat must always keep clear of the leeward boat.

In both these cases, even if there is not a collision but the innocent party has to alter course, it is still an offence. The guilty party has to take a penalty turn, which is two circles. If he doesn't, the innocent party is entitled to protest the offending boat. It then goes to a protest jury. There are normally five jury members. Both sailors state their case. You are entitled to have witnesses, and the jury can ask questions. The sailors are sent away and the jury deliberates.

However, it should be stressed that, even if you have the right of way, you must give the other boat the opportunity to keep clear. The former can't, at the last minute, change course and hit the other boat. Inevitably, sometimes decisions are very tight, and very difficult to adjudicate.

One area that commonly causes a dispute is when you approach a racing mark, there is a three-boat-length zone. Once the front boat reaches that, if there's an overlap, the outside boat has to let the inside boat pass round the mark first. He has the right to ask the outside boat to give him room. Sometimes it's difficult to judge if there's an overlap. It causes a few arguments.

Those are the basic rules. It gets a lot worse. Some rules are quite subtle. They are just something you have to get used to; and learn what you can and can't do. Sometimes it's a grey area. You can argue about it on the water, and sometimes just take the penalty anyway, to be safe, and still protest the other boat. Sometimes it does go to protest. I've had quite a few of those over the years. It's like a footballer and the offside rule. Sometimes you will get the decision; sometimes not. You have to know when the cards are in your favour and you can push it. It's a big part of competitive sailing.

The jury members are ex-sailors, all amateurs. They do it for their love of the sport. And it's an incredibly tough job. It's easy to get frustrated with them. Sometimes these things happen so quickly, it's hard for them. Look at Rule 42, which concerns the amount of effort you can put into working the boat. There are very tight rules about how much you can play the sails and use your body weight to move the boat. And that is a highly subjective rule. All the sailors are constantly on the edge of that. You work the boat as fast as it will go, but you can only do it so much before you start breaking the rules. It's the toughest thing to judge.

Downwind, in the Finn, above 15 knots you can do whatever you like; you can rock the boat, pump the sails to catch the waves as much as you like because it's physically harder. In light winds, if you were allowed to do that, it would just become a bit of a joke, to be honest. Under 15 knots, in the Finn, you can only pump the sail once per wave and you're not allowed to use your body weight to rock the boat. Upwind you're not permitted to jerk your body to flip the sail or flip the rig to make it go quicker. In windy conditions, you're allowed to go for it. It does become very physical. In light winds it just wouldn't be sailing. You'd just be fanning the boat along.

Every now and again, someone goes too far, gets a flag and has to do a penalty turn. It's happened to me. It can be frustrating. You have to work with the umpires to try and get an idea how they're thinking, how they're judging it. If you get a second flag, you get disqualified from that race. If you get a third flag, you're disqualified from the whole event.

Returning to that second race at Athens, these were the circumstances. On the first windward leg, the Frenchman Florent and I were both far out on the left-hand corner of the track, which was the favoured side, coming up to the top mark. We were both so far on our own that no other boats were around. Not even the jury boat. I was on the port tack, which is the 'give way' tack. He was coming on starboard tack. So, he had the right of way. But as I've explained, under the rules you can't just sail up at the last minute and try and hit someone; you have to give them the opportunity to keep clear.

I crossed well ahead of him and, as far as I was concerned, there was no issue. I stayed clear of him. However, at the last minute, he started screaming at me, luffed towards me and I thought he was going to hit me. I gave him a hard time, because he was bang out of order. I said: 'Mate, what are you doing?' He appeared to want to placate me, and said something to the effect of: 'Oh, I'm sorry. I'm being an a*******. Don't worry about it.'

I thought: 'OK, fine. We'll leave it at that.'

I didn't think I'd done anything wrong but if he had said 'Oh, I'm going to protest,' I'd have done a '720', a penalty turn. Not because I believed I was at fault, but to protect myself from the very thing that happened. But he didn't. His behaviour in that respect still infuriates me to this day.

There is an etiquette to this. In the old days, if you wanted to protest, you used to have to fly a red flag. In crewed boats, like the America's Cup, you still fly a flag. But in single-handed racing, they changed the rule a number of years ago to say that you do not have to fly a flag, just shout 'Protest.' But who's to know if you've done that?

I had to go back for the protest hearing. Florent had no witnesses. I didn't either. No other sailors were in the vicinity. Basically it was his word against mine. But as he was the starboard-tack boat, all the onus in the protest was on me, on port tack, to prove that nothing ever happened. I had crossed ahead of him. Though it was really close, there was no contact, even though he had tried to come up and hit me. His account was that he had to bear away. I was disqualified. As it can be imagined, I was furious.

I can hear people saying: 'Well, you've been in similar situations before, but in reverse, like in Sydney, against Robert Scheidt.' But that was a completely different situation. To me, it was obvious what I was doing in that Sydney finale, and that it was within the rules. I didn't try to conceal it. If Florent had seriously felt I had infringed the rules here, he should have shouted 'Protest' when I crossed. Though, frankly, I would still have felt it was purely gamesmanship, I could have done a penalty turn. I couldn't get my head around what happened.

The upshot was that, after two races, I was twenty-fourth overall. At the time, with Kusznierewicz getting off to a flying start, I really felt my Games were over. The actions of that one man could deny me a gold medal.

Indeed when I came down to the boat park the next morning, I sensed that a lot of my rivals had little smirks on their faces. Here I was, favourite, but at the time placed twenty-fourth, and the other sailors were glancing at me with a look that said: 'You're out of it, mate.' They were loving this. And it was true. I was not in a good situation. I just thought to myself: 'OK guys . . .'

I was written off. None of the media, or my rivals, gave me a chance. Though I had come good before from a poor start, there are not very good starts, and there are completely disastrous starts!

It was like I had to start again after that first day. Despite my basic belief in myself, I knew I'd have to sail the best I'd ever sailed to have a chance. I resolved to use that first day's experience positively. I used it to motivate myself. I was determined to prove to my rivals that I was still the best. I was so fired up.

I needed to be one hundred per cent focussed, so I decided to keep my own counsel. I didn't speak to the press at all for the rest of the regatta. In that respect, I was helped by the so-called Three Blondes in a Boat, Shirley Robertson and the two Sarahs, Ayton and Webb, drawing away much of the attention that could have been directed towards me. And the fact that Matthew Pinsent was rowing to his fourth gold on the Saturday. That meant I could quietly get on with repairing the damage of that first day.

In fact, I watched Matthew's race on TV first thing on that Saturday. We had the BBC feed, with an English commentary, which was good. It was an awesome performance by Matt and his crew, though another nail-biter. But that really helped to inspire me, too. You take a lot from watching other Brits do well at an Olympics. The same applied in Beijing when the road cyclist Nicole Cooke secured Britain's first gold there.

The next two days were really breezy, which was fortunate.

It suited me. They were conditions for really aggressive sailing. It was fantastic. I could really take out on the boat all my indignation at what Florent had done to my chances – and really go for it. I had two firsts on that second day. I remember overtaking the Belgian competitor, Godefroid, on the last reach to the finish which is something you hardly ever do – in fact, he appeared so surprised, he ended up capsizing! – and I crossed the finish line, looked back at all the other guys and just said to myself: 'F★★★ the lot of you . . .' It was a pretty big declaration to the rest of the fleet that I wasn't just going to lie down and roll over.

That was followed by another first and a fourth the following day, after which I was back into the overall lead. As far as Florent was concerned, I'd never been so angry in my entire life. I didn't say anything, or do anything. I didn't have to. He must have known how I felt. I remember sailing near him the next day, and he was probably paranoid that I was going to come after him and take him out which can't have helped his concentration. But I wasn't going to nobble him. I was just focussed on my own series and it just clicked. I got in the flow, I was sailing fast, getting good starts and making the right tactical calls.

By the end of the series of races, it was all somewhat anti-climactic. The final race was a poor one because there was barely any wind. To claim the gold, I just needed to finish within twelve places of the Spanish sailor, Rafael Trujillo. I had a nice start to the race, and was in great control. Then I made a really bad mistake in the first windward leg. At one point there was a danger that it was actually going to be quite close. I had a bit of a sweat on for the first half of the race. But I did manage to catch up with Rafa, the Spaniard, and get back in front of him, making life a lot easier.

There was no immediate surge of delight. It all happened very slowly. Though it may sound strange, I had been more concerned on the last leg by the fact that whatever I did could possibly decide the destination of the bronze and the silver. It was really close between Rafa and Mateusz Kusznierewicz for second and third. To ensure I was going to win, I didn't exactly slow Rafa down, but I didn't really help him, either. I ended up with an awful dilemma. Because I'd held Rafa up, should I then let him past on the final leg to kind of even things up? Or was that not really fair because that could affect Kusznierewicz's finishing position? I was placed in this unenviable position of playing God.

I did what I thought was correct. As it transpired, I had no impact on the outcome. So, afterwards I felt much better about it. But at the time, I was really upset because I thought 'Shit, I might have just made the difference here. Is that fair, or not?' It really troubled me. The fact that I'd just won a gold medal was inconsequential. It sounds bizarre, but I was more worried about the destination of silver and bronze.

I had finally begun to wind down by the time I was presented with my gold medal by the IOC president, Jacques Rogge, who's an ex-Finn sailor himself. It was particularly satisfying when he remarked: 'From one Finn sailor to another.' I was pretty chuffed by that endorsement. Later that year, I would be awarded an OBE. That was a fantastic moment for me, but probably meant as much to my parents, who'd supported me all the way.

Sailing is such a complex sport. So much goes into it; the boat set-up, wind conditions and an element of luck sometimes. You have to deal with it all. Then there are the rules, and, of course, how other competitors may be acting. As I've already indicated, racing can be very aggressive sometimes. It's a lot to cope with, and there are so many ups and downs. That's why experience comes into it. You have to be very level-headed about the fact that you are going to get it wrong at times and fall back a number of places. That's the nature of the game. It's impossible to get it right one hundred per cent of the time.

Conversely, when it does come right, the sense of satisfaction is all the more intense.

The great thing about the Games is sailing under the Union flag. Receiving a gold, and hearing the national anthem being played is an incredibly proud moment. That's what makes the Olympics so special. It also brings sports like sailing, where there's a relative lack of knowledge, compared to track and field, to the fore. People can relate to your achievement.

In the second week, I went out and watched Iain Percy and Steve Mitchell racing in the Star class. They had a really tough regatta, and eventually finished sixth. After things had gone well for me, that was really difficult for me to watch because of Iain being a great mate. It was hard to know how to deal with that, how to support them. Half of me thought 'Well, they probably don't want to see me around. They're still trying to race.' But the other half felt I should be more supportive.

I learnt a lot from that because it was the same situation in Beijing. I was racing in the first week, while my friends Iain and Bart were competing in the Star class in the second. In fact, at Beijing, we went and played golf one day when we had a day off. But otherwise I just stayed off the water, and tried to be as supportive as possible on shore.

Meanwhile, of course, Shirley Robertson and her crew had won gold. I was delighted for Shirley. I have huge admiration for her because she's done it the hard way. She started off in the

Barcelona 1992 Olympics, when she finished ninth in the Europe class, just missed out in 1996, when she finished fourth, which was incredibly hard for her. Yet, she persevered, came back at Sydney, and won the gold. It was hard moving into the three-woman keelboat, the Yngling class. On her own, she was so single-minded, and had such a high work ethic. So, it was sometimes hard for the other two girls. They must have learnt a huge amount from sailing with Shirley. They were far and away the best team at those Games and deserved their triumph.

In certain sports, there's an imbalance of medals available to men and women. I think sailing has it right in that respect – certainly in Olympic terms. In other areas of the sport, it's not easy for women to break through at times, though they certainly make up for that in global challenges, the most famous being Dame Ellen MacArthur. But there is encouragement. In the youth world championships, there are a lot of girls' classes. I'd say it's a pretty inclusive sport where people from any background, or any age, can be out there racing and having fun.

Chapter 11

Perils at Sea

When I first tried out Iain Percy's old Finn, under David Howlett's guidance, back in 2002, I was stepping into the unknown slightly. I guess there was a risk that I wouldn't have taken to the new class of boat, but in a way that made it all the more exciting and gave me the motivation to make it a success. I've always sought a rich variety of sailing experiences, new challenges. It really appealed to me when, after the Athens Olympics, I was offered the chance to take part in one of *the* great races, the Sydney to Hobart race. I'd always relished the idea of ocean racing, and swiftly I discovered how exhilarating, and, indeed, potentially perilous it can be. Conditions can be treacherous, even for experienced sailors.

Neville Crichton invited me to be one of the helmsmen on his 'Shockwave' maxi yacht, named *Alfa Romeo,* in the 2005 renewal of the race. Neville, an Australian-based Kiwi who is a very successful businessman, is now a good friend, whom I've sailed with many times. Of the yachts which started out on Boxing Day on the 628 nautical-mile race, Neville's was the biggest and fastest maxi, along with her sister ship, *Wild Oats XI,* owned by Bob Oatley, a wealthy wine merchant. We had a great duel with those guys. It ended up a really close race in notoriously bad conditions.

I'm not frightened of the sea, or the conditions you can find yourself in, but you must retain a healthy respect. I should admit at this point that, at the best of times, I'm not a particularly good swimmer. I do try really hard to stay out of the water! In most Olympic racing, you have to wear a life jacket all the time. The Finn, which is quite a big boat, is an exception. When there's a light wind that rule's not enforced. In races like the Sydney-Hobart, you also wear a harness. Or should do.

However, even that may not be enough. It didn't save Glyn Charles, a sailor I knew well, and whose death ensured I will never, ever be complacent.

Glyn was one of the characters who really helped me at the Atlanta Games in 1996. He competed in the Star class in the Olympic team, and was an incredibly nice, genuine fellow, and a great sailor. He was someone I had really looked up to. He and Adrian Stead really took me under their wing, and they were the people I'd have a chat to if I had any problems.

He had been spending a month or two racing in Australia over the Christmas and New Year of 1998 and was the tactician on a yacht, *Sword of Orion*, with mostly Aussie sailors in the Sydney to Hobart. There were hurricane conditions, and the waves were so rough due to the strong ocean currents running between Australia and Tasmania. The smaller boats, of which *Sword of Orion* was one, were battered the hardest and so Glyn and his team decided to try and sail back to Eden on the Australian mainland.

The boat was hit by a huge wave, which rolled the boat over. Glyn was on the helm at the time. One other guy was on deck; the rest were down below. The boom broke and crashed across the boat. It knocked Glyn into the water. No one's sure precisely what happened, but though he had his harness clipped on, it appears it broke. He was badly injured, so he couldn't get back on to the boat. Someone tried to tie a rope to themselves, and jump in and get out to him, but couldn't make it. Glynn was one of the last people you'd ever expect to be lost like that. He was such an experienced sailor who had done a lot of offshore sailing.

Glyn wasn't the only victim in what turned out to be a horrendous 1998 race. Of the 115 yachts which started out from Sydney Harbour on 26 December only forty-four made it to Hobart. Five boats sank and sixty-six boats retired from the race. Six sailors died and fifty-five were taken off their yachts by helicopter.

Knowing Glyn so well made it that much worse. It was shocking for the sport to lose Glyn after John Merricks had died, albeit in different circumstances, the previous year. It's true what they say. The good die young.

It would be remiss of me not to add an addendum to their deaths. At the Sydney Olympics, there was more than a touch of poignancy about the Olympic silver medal won in the Star by GB's Mark Covell and Ian Walker.

Mark had originally planned to campaign the Star with Glyn Charles. In the event, Mark got together with Ian, whose own lifelong sailing partner and Olympic co-medallist John Merricks had died in that 1997 car crash in the mountains of Italy. John and Ian had been driving to a restaurant for the prize-giving, after a regatta based in Punta Ala, when the four-wheel drive in which they were passengers rolled over on a hairpin bend. Ian escaped, but John was thrown out of the vehicle and was killed.

Ian and Mark decided to form a partnership after the former's consoling phone call regarding Glyn's death. As Mark reportedly explained, following the Sydney medal ceremony: 'Originally it wasn't about sailing together but I really did want to carry on – but only with somebody who could match up to Glyn.'

The potential dangers are something you have to be aware of. But sailing with good teams and having professional, experienced sailors around you makes a huge difference. And you must always, always, be switched on to the dangers. It's easy to get too comfortable in the situation, and take things for granted. The next thing you know, you're in trouble. When things go wrong there is always a chain of events and it's critical to try not to compound difficult situations with rash decision-making.

Returning to my own Sydney to Hobart debut, on the second night out, it got really rough in the Bass Strait. There was about 35 knots of breeze, downwind, full sail up. It was wild. The first time I'd really experienced that. We blew out four spinnakers. I was just there for the experience. And what an experience it was!

I remember at one time being up on the bow, helping the bowman Joey Allen, who's very well known in the sailing world, a real old sea dog. He had won a couple of America's Cups and a couple of Whitbread races. There was just the pair of us, and this boat tearing along doing about 30mph. I was thinking 'What the hell am I doing up here?' Joey was just shouting orders and telling me to hang on.

I remember one particular moment. It was the middle of the night, pitch black, I was at the back of the boat, and we gybed down this wave. That's when a boat is at its quickest. It's when the boat is easiest to control, because it takes the pressure off the sails. We actually nosedived, and the helmsman put the bow under the wave in front. The boat went from doing 30 knots to 8 knots. It's like slamming on the brakes in a car. The pressure of water just blew back through the pulpit of the boat. That blew the spinnaker back, ripping it in two, all the way up; just destroyed the sail.

Joey was actually up on the bow, without a harness on. Unbelievable. We all thought that he'd be washed away by the incredible force of the water. In fact, he'd seen what was about to happen, and free-climbed up the forestay, which took some doing. The water had rushed past underneath him. His instincts saved him. Normally, you'd have a harness on; but it's difficult in those boats because there's so much going on, and it impedes your movement.

By the finish of the race, we had taken a bit of a battering. We eventually finished second, beaten by the other maxi, *Wild Oats XI*, which reached Hobart in what proved to be a record time of 1 hour 18 minutes 40 seconds. It was a very quick race.

Overall, it's a reasonably safe sport, although there have been instances where beginners have got swept out to sea. But offshore sailing obviously can be particularly dangerous. Only last year (2008), the French skipper Yann Eliès broke his leg in the Vendée Globe, the single-handed, non-stop, round-the-world race, and had to be rescued by an Australian navy frigate. It was the Australian navy who also came to the aid of the Briton Tony Bullimore who in the '97 Vendée Globe capsized in the Southern Ocean. He survived inside his upturned boat for five days.

Fortunately, I haven't experienced anything like that. Yet.

In more light-hearted vein, I have had my less than glorious moments on the water. One of the most embarrassing was when

I was involved in the America's Cup Jubilee Regatta in 2001 at Cowes. All the top boats in the world were there. We were racing in the maxi class. I was helming a 100ft supermaxi, *Leopard*, owned by Mike Slade, a flamboyant yachtsman who made his fortune from property investments. Like me, he had started out on dinghies in Cornwall when he was a young boy. His passion, though, was for the biggest, most powerful yachts.

It was the first time I had sailed anything that size. At the time, because I was involved with the OneWorld America's Cup team, Peter Gilmour was in charge of the boat, doing the tactics, and trying to talk me through it. There was a very crowded start line. Basically we were there early and were attempting to get back behind the line.

We had come round and were aiming for a gap between two yachts. One of them suddenly stopped and the opening just disappeared. We had nowhere to go. There was a horrible inevitability about what happened next. Another yacht, an 80-footer called *Morning Glory*, had powered off the start line, probably doing about 12 knots. We were doing a similar speed, going across them. They T-boned us, rammed right into the side of us. I remember it vividly. They hit us just past where I was standing, steering the boat.

Morning Glory was owned by Hasso Plattner, the US-based billionaire German entrepreneur who was one of the founders of SAP, the software giant.

There had been loads of shouting and screaming from the other boat. It was an almighty collision, and it virtually ripped the bow off *Morning Glory*. To give you an idea, the damaged boat reminded me of a cross-channel ferry, with its bow up. It looked ridiculous. However, because the damage was above the waterline they carried on racing – as did we. Our boat was damaged too, but not quite as badly. We restarted the race, but it was the worst feeling I'd ever had on a boat. I looked at Mike Slade, the owner, who was sitting in the cockpit, staring at the floor in disbelief. He was speechless. His daughter was on board, and she was really upset.

Sure, they could have done a better job at avoiding us. But it was a start-line collision and we were the boat in the wrong. I had to accept that. It was my fault. I felt so bad. I just had to get away as far as possible, and sort myself out.

After a while I said to Peter Gilmour 'You'd better take over for a bit.'

So, I went up to the bow, which on that boat was a hell of a way forward, and sat next to the bowman. I said: 'F★★★.'

He said: 'What's happened?'

I replied: 'Didn't you see?'

He shook his head. He hadn't even realised what had taken place. I explained the circumstances. 'Don't worry about it,' he tried to console me. 'It'll be fine.'

I thought: 'Yeah, right.'

After about five minutes, I had calmed myself down, and returned to the helm. Peter Gilmour was actually really good about it. He said: 'Don't worry. It's happened to me loads of times.'

He was being very kind. It was obviously a really bad situation, and potentially quite dangerous. Someone could have got hurt. Also, and this immediately crossed my mind, it would have involved hundreds of thousands of pounds' worth of damage. These supermaxis are the most powerful and expensive sailing yachts around, and can cost millions of pounds. The best you could say was that it was a good learning experience, albeit an expensive one.

Though both boats still continued racing, as ours had been responsible for the collision, we took the decision to retire from the race just before the finish.

It was hugely embarrassing for me. After the race, Mike said: 'Look, I think we'd better go and speak to Hasso.'

This was a major event, with enormous crowds. Hasso had a big SAP corporate marquee on the island. We entered. It was completely silent. There was a chair in the far corner. You could make out someone sitting there, with a cigar, and smoke wafting up. One of his acolytes was standing next to him. It was like something out of a Bond movie.

Hasso said nothing, but his sidekick started laying into me.

'This is ridiculous. Who are you? You could have killed someone. Don't you realise how dangerous that is?' And so he continued.

Then Hasso turned round, and said: 'What is your name?'

'My name's Ben Ainslie.'

'Who are you? What have you done? What are you trying to do to me? Everyone always tries to do this to me.'

Fortunately, Mike intervened. He was very laid-back, the archetypal English gentleman, who could ooze charm. He said 'Oh, Hasso, darling. Terribly sorry. Anything we can do.' That kind of thing. He was fantastic and did a really good job of calming the waters, so to speak. Hasso's wrath was eventually assuaged, just about.

Since then I've actually raced a lot against Hasso, including in the maxi world championships only a couple of years ago when I was sailing with Neville Crichton. The boats would dock next to each other. He saw me, and shouted: 'You! I remember you from the Jubilee Regatta.'

I tried to make light of it. 'Oh, yes . . . but you didn't really like that boat, anyway. You've got a better boat now.'

'I loved that boat,' he protested. 'It was the best boat I ever had, and you ruined it.' Fortunately, his manner cooled, and he added: 'But I've been watching you, and you've been doing really well in the Finn, so keep it up.' We were over the worst.

Cowes was the scene of another accident I was involved in before the Beijing Olympics. To make matters worse, the Formula 1 driver Lewis Hamilton, who was bidding for the championship, was on board.

The Round the Island race, sponsored by JP Morgan Asset Management, is one of the biggest participation races in the world, so there were thousands of boats out there.

We were on the British solo sailor Alex Thomson's Hugo Boss boat, a new Open 60. Boss are also big sponsors of McLaren. It was a boat designed and developed for the 2008–9 Vendée Globe, though unfortunately, Alex would have to pull out of the race because of a cracked hull.

Lewis was on a tight schedule. He had been to the Nelson Mandela concert the night before in Hyde Park, and the race starts at 6 a.m. So, he got a helicopter down at four in the morning and climbed on board about five minutes before the race started.

He was all starry-eyed. He had his BlackBerry out and was taking pictures of everything. Meanwhile Alex was steering the boat. We came together with two other yachts. Alex made a desperate manoeuvre to try and get out of the situation. In doing so, the bowsprit of his yacht took out the backstay of another boat which caused its mast to fall down. It also ripped the bowsprit off Alex's yacht.

It was a major collision. All of a sudden, Lewis' BlackBerry was back in his pocket! It all went very quiet. It's nothing like an F1 smash at over 100mph, of course, but he suddenly realised this was quite serious. Poor Alex was devastated. It was a terrible thing to happen. He thought he'd have to pull out of the race which would have been decidedly unfortunate as it was all part of a big PR angle for Hugo Boss. I persuaded Alex we could still race. The only issue was going downwind. Normally, you'd fly the spinnaker off the bowsprit, but this meant we had to fly it off the bow.

So, we got on with the race. Conditions were great. There was a good breeze, and Lewis didn't need any persuading to have a go at the helm. It was really impressive to watch him. People who haven't sailed before are a bit wobbly to start off with; they tend to get very easily distracted. Also, you have to bear in mind that he was surrounded by loads of TV cameramen filming his every move.

He took five minutes to familiarise himself, get used to it, but after that he was so focussed; he understood all the numbers on the boat, the boat speed and the wind angles. He wasn't distracted by all the other boats. I've got to admit that I'd relish the chance to swap with him. I love driving and karting. There's obviously a similar focus about our sports – if not the speed.

Anyway, we went through The Needles, round to the back of the island, and got the spinnaker up. We had an awesome ride, 25 knots. We had a really good race with Mike Golding, and managed to stay ahead and win the race in the Open 60.

During the race, I wondered what life was like for a man who has every facet of his life scrutinised and pored over. He is certainly very professional at doing what he has to do for the sponsors, and is pretty mature for his age. I guess he's got to be, really, in that position. He also has to be very careful what he says, in the knowledge that things can be taken out of context, or words can be manipulated to give a different impression from that intended.

Alex and I went to the British Grand Prix six weeks later, as guests of McLaren. We went to the pits and saw Lewis before the race. He knows Alex quite well because of the Hugo Boss link. Lewis was on great form and seemed very confident about the race which he went on to dominate. After the race we ended up in the team motorhome with all the sponsors and friends of the team. I was hugely impressed by the accessibility of F1 and how well they promoted the sport whilst still maintaining a quality competition for the drivers. It is something sailing could certainly learn from. When you look at the America's Cup it has the potential to be the sailing equivalent of F1.

To a degree, I can identify with someone who's so busy, and who goes to functions and shows and feels like they're being paraded. You just have to be very courteous, very nice to everyone, asking the right questions, even if not all of the answers actually register. A bit like a politician, I guess. I get that occasionally. For Lewis, it must be most days.

The prang in the Round the Island race was unfortunate but it wasn't my responsibility, I have to stress. However, there was one other infamous occasion when things didn't quite work out for me on the water, and which still provokes some embarrassment for me, and Iain Percy.

Iain and I had come to two private agreements regarding the 1994 youth national championships. Basically, the one who *didn't* win would compete in the youth match-racing championships. The guy who *did* win would crew for him in the three-man boat. So, after I had returned from the youth world championships, Iain, his brother, Richard, and I took part in our first match-racing event at one of the reservoirs near Heathrow.

Though we sailed quite well, we struggled a bit because we had absolutely no idea what the rules were. We were nearly disqualified for abusing the umpires, because we could not understand the rules.

Another agreement that Iain and I had was that after the '96 Olympics we would sail in the Laser 5000 national championships at Hayling Island. That was then a relatively new class, with a new type of boat. They were much faster and more dynamic, and harder to sail if you weren't used to them.

They were twin trapeze (a wire used in high-performance boats that enables sailors to place their weight further outside the boat than just by sitting out). It meant that you'd both have to use the trapeze wire. Neither of us had used them before.

It had large asymmetrical sails. Again we'd never sailed anything like that before. But we trained for a week, and each day improved and became a little bit more confident. The day before the regatta started, there was quite a good breeze, about 15–20 knots. It was a really nice sunny day, but no one was going out sailing. We couldn't understand why. But we were determined to go out. We needed a bit more practice in the breeze.

Out in the bay, it got up to about 20 knots. But we were doing fine. It was an awesome day for sailing. We had a good session and decided to come back in. It was downwind back into the harbour entrance at Hayling Island. There's a big sandbar and it gets very rough at certain states of the tide, particularly when it's flowing out of the harbour, which it was then. You get quite big overhanging waves.

Anyway, we were flying back in, enjoying ourselves, but then we launched off this wave, and pitch-poled the boat (in other words the bow lands and then the boat keeps going over, stern over the bow). Both Iain and I went flying off. It was very funny at the time but we soon realised that the water was too shallow and the boat was being smashed up on the sandbar. It meant the mast broke on the seabed, the sails were ripped and the rudder was damaged.

I have to admit, and bearing in mind our age – I was only around 19 at the time, Iain a year older – that our first reaction was to laugh, and mostly at ourselves; it was a pretty impressive wipeout.

We swam back to the boat, and somehow got it upright. But then we began to realise what damage we'd done to a borrowed boat. Probably about £8,000 worth, although fortunately it was insured. Not only that, we also had to get back to the sailing club which was about two miles down the harbour.

We could easily have made our own way back, although it would have taken a long time. However, someone had obviously seen it all happen from the beach, and had called out the inshore lifeboat from its base at the lifeboat, just a rigid inflatable, the end of Chichester Harbour. We were not in danger, but they towed us back into Hayling Island Sailing Club.

That, I should explain, is quite a large facility, with balconies overlooking the harbour. No one else was sailing. They were all back at the club. They saw us getting towed and, bearing in mind this was about two weeks after I'd won a silver medal at the Olympics, we returned to a standing ovation. It was right up there with the America's Cup Jubilee Regatta in terms of humiliation. It's not something I'll be allowed to forget

The organisers very kindly got us a new boat and sent it down. We fixed it up, went out racing, and took part in the event.

Chapter 12

Back into America's Cup Contention

I had been training for the world championships in Cadiz, in 2003, when the America's Cup appeared on my radar once more. Dean Barker, skipper of the Emirates Team New Zealand boat, called me up. He said they were trying to put a team together for the next Cup in 2007, and asked if I'd be interested in getting involved as a member of the afterguard.

It immediately appealed to me, though Team New Zealand had been beset by difficulties since its successful years of 1995 and 2000.

I should explain a little of the history of the team. Sir Peter Blake, a Kiwi yachting legend, and the first to win the Whitbread Round the World race, was the syndicate head who had galvanised Team New Zealand's America's Cup team to win it in 1995 and 2000, under skipper Russell Coutts. But that all changed in the ensuing years, for two reasons.

First, Coutts and his tactician Brad Butterworth had decided on a new challenge with the Swiss challenger, Alinghi. Then, in 2001, Blake was murdered by pirates at the mouth of the

Amazon in Brazil while documentary-making. Blake's long-term friend and rival, Grant Dalton, was brought in to take over his mantle. His exploits in offshore racing and particularly in the Whitbread, which he won in 1993–4, had elevated him to celebrity status in his native New Zealand.

Meanwhile with Coutts and Brad Butterworth no longer with the team, Dean Barker had taken over as skipper.

Dean had been involved with Team New Zealand since 1995, when Russell Coutts invited him to train with them. By the time of the team's 2000 successful defence, he was regarded so highly that Coutts had handed over the skipper's role to him for the last race.

Unfortunately, in 2003, Team New Zealand, skippered and helmed by Dean, had been defeated 5-0 in the final by the challenger, Alinghi. It was the first time the Cup had returned to Europe in 152 years, and was considered something approaching a national disgrace back home in New Zealand. It led to all manner of incrimination. Coutts and Butterworth also received a barrage of abuse from their fellow countrymen, many of whom saw the duo as traitors.

The team was in tatters. It was totally demoralised and had no funding. But Grant Dalton did a fantastic job in encouraging back the core people who needed to stay in the team. Then he needed to bring in a whole new group of people to help take it to the next level. That was when Dean got in touch with me. He told me that Grant was coming to Cadiz and wanted to meet up.

I met Grant for a drink before the racing started. I was wary and apprehensive, after what had happened with the OneWorld project. I still felt pretty raw after that experience. Yet, there was no way that my sailing career was going to include one America's Cup, from which I'd walked away, with people saying: 'Oh, he's not a team player. He's never going to be successful at that side of the sport.'

I'd always had it in my mind that I'd go back to the America's Cup one day, and make a success of it. I wanted to see the positive side of the America's Cup, for my own sake, to prove that I could do it.

I was relieved to discover that Dalton was a completely straightforward guy. In fact, I'd describe him as a pit bull terrier on speed. Totally direct and no-nonsense, though I also found his approach quite amusing, in a way.

He used expressions like: 'This is bullshit.' 'They f***** that up.' 'This is where the money's coming from.' 'I'm getting these, or those, sponsors.' And, most pertinent, where I was concerned, was the directness of this issue: 'I want you to do this job.'

That job was to be the strategist on the race boat. That is the guy who looks for the wind, and basically helps the tactician make the decisions on where to go. He also wanted me to do the match-racing circuit with Dean, as part of his crew, and also with my own crew. And also do some helming on the B boat, the second boat.

To me, that America's Cup invitation sounded like the perfect scenario. I wanted to be on the race boat, the 'first team' boat, and strategist was a good role. That would work for me. But I also wanted to learn how to match-race, and helm America's Cup boats.

The concept really appealed to me. So did Grant's character. And his vision. Neither did it escape my thinking that Team New Zealand has so much history in the America's Cup from 1987 onwards, with the pinnacle coming in '95 and 2000, when they won the Cup.

Many things drew me to the team. Ever since I was a youngster, and went down there with the Laser Radials, I had been in awe of the New Zealand sailing set-up. Kiwi yachting was the pre-eminent force in offshore sailing, via the Whitbread and the America's Cup, from the early nineties onwards. I wanted to be part of that.

There *were* still people involved from those earlier Team New Zealand campaigns, so they had a lot of experience. There were great sailors like Tony Ray, a lovely guy, who had won the Whitbread Round the World race a couple of times and the America's Cup twice; the vastly experienced Joey Allen, who I've mentioned before, a character who'd been around for decades. There was the afterguard coach, Rod Davis, an American by birth, but who had married a Kiwi. He had sailed with Team New Zealand in America's Cups since '92 and was also an Olympic gold medallist, with a gold in the Soling class at Los Angeles '84, and a silver in the Star at Barcelona '92 . It was a great attraction for me to work with him.

Meanwhile I had qualified for the Athens Games at the world championships in Cadiz. That October, Grant Dalton rang me to see if I was still interested in his proposal. I said I was. We talked about money. He also said that Dean Barker was due to take part in a match-racing event out in Bermuda – one of the big five regattas of the year – and did I want to go out and crew for him in a four-man boat? I agreed, went out there, and we got on really well. Other members of the crew were Tony Ray, who was on the mainsheet, and James Dagg, who was trimming. I was on the bow, which was quite a new position for me, and doing the tactics as well. It all came together, and we performed well in the event – despite my terrible work on the bow!

Anyway, I agreed to join the team once I'd finished with the

Athens Olympics the following summer. Nothing much would happen for twelve months.

My relationship with Dean Barker started off well. We talked a lot about the Olympics, and that actually encouraged him to do a Finn campaign in the year before Athens. The next thing, he came over to Europe and trained with me, at La Linea in Spain, together with the Spanish Olympic representative, Rafael Trujillo, who ended up winning the silver. Dean qualified for the Athens Olympics in the Finn, but had a tough regatta finishing outside the medals.

After the Olympics, I joined up with Team New Zealand. The team competed in a number of preliminary regattas throughout Europe between 2004 and 2007. They are known as the 'Acts'. They were very useful, allowing us to race and fine-tune the team, and also counted towards the seeding for the challenger selection series, the Louis Vuitton Cup, which followed. I got my chance at the helm of the race boat in the final event, Act 13, and got on really well with the majority of the team; certainly the Kiwis, who were all great guys.

The afterguard on the race boat – the first team, so to speak – consisted of Dean, who was steering and skippering the boat (he concentrated on working with the trimmers and looking forward); Terry Hutchinson, a very successful professional sailor from the US who was the tactician, and with whom I would have to work closely; and Adam Beashel, the guy who went up the rig and looked for wind. I knew Adam quite well already. He's brilliant sailor and we got on fine. Kevin Hall was the navigator and had also been at OneWorld.

I should explain, at this stage, how the roles work. Much is self-explanatory, but the helmsman steers to get the boat moving as fast as he can. He works with trimmers to get the sails trimmed properly. Things happen so quickly that a lot of it is intuitive, to get the right position and best start you can. He works with the rest of the crew about manoeuvres that are coming up, with the mark-roundings and approaches to the marks. He also takes information from the tactician, who is responsible for where the boat is on the course, and what he thinks is the best manoeuvre compared to the other boats, and with the prevailing wind conditions.

He works a lot in tandem with the strategist, who looks for wind – together, often, with a guy up the mast who searches for dark water, and cloud, which are key signs. It's a crucial area. There is a weather team on shore who, before the race starts, give an idea of what the wind will be doing.

The afterguard also includes a navigator, who uses a computer display of the course. That group at the back of the boat all work together. In a major event, there can be a lot of stress and tension on board. It has to be a very tight unit. Everyone must get on very well together.

Our schedule was split into match-racing and fleet-racing. We proceeded to go through the match-racing series, and that all went very well. We won that; then went into the fleet-racing series. As I've said, I was the strategist on the race boat for those Acts, as they are called. It wasn't an auspicious start. In the second race we were over the start line. So, we had to go back. We were at the rear of the fleet and had a really tough race. I mentioned something to Terry at what must have been the wrong time. He then spent the whole race in my ear complaining that I had put him off his game. I thought we should have just focussed on the race and discussed the issues afterwards. It was clear our styles were different.

Chapter 13

Tensions Eased as Team Builds Towards Cup

If there was one thing I had learnt from my experience at OneWorld it was to act if something was not right. Rather that than bury my head in the sand and hope it would all work out. Grant and I chatted over the phone about it over the next couple of weeks, and it was agreed that I would helm the B boat instead of doing the strategy role. It worked well for the team as Ray Davies, another very talented Kiwi sailor, moved into my former role as strategist and did a brilliant job. However, the way the move was put across by Grant publicly, it was more that I was going to be an opponent of Dean.

According to press reports, Grant was going to give me a shot at helming the B boat, with the implication that if I could beat Dean, I might end up being the skipper of the race boat. It wasn't necessarily what I wanted. I just wanted to learn over those two years – how to match-race and how to helm the big boats.

At the time I was concerned I had possibly made the wrong call. A sailing journalist who I get on well with was in town and invited me to play golf one afternoon along with Russell Coutts. I remember chatting with Russell about it and he felt pretty strongly that I had done the right thing if I wanted to be helming in the future. It was a relief to hear those words and I enjoyed the opportunity to pick his brains for a couple of hours.

Another guy who was extraordinarily helpful was a New Zealander, Kelvin Harrap, a highly experienced sailor, who was originally supposed to be the B-boat helmsman. A member of the Kiwis' '96 Olympic sailing team, in the Soling class, and a veteran of two Whitbreads, this was Kelvin's fourth America's Cup. He'd also been involved with TAG Heuer (1995), America True (2000) and the OneWorld Challenge (2003) of which, of course, I had also briefly been part.

Kelvin ended up being the tactician on the B boat and we became good friends and worked well together. Kelvin is pretty relaxed but a very experienced sailor and so it was perfect to have his advice and tactical calls. Our job was to sail the boat flat out in the two-boat testing session and also to push Dean and the race team in our in-house racing sessions.

I was really fortunate that Kelvin dealt with it the way he did. We were able to move forward and build a good team amongst the guys on the B boat down in Auckland where we were based. There was a lot of incentive for them. You have to remember that several members of the B crew were determined to make it to the race boat. Indeed, some were quite bitter they weren't on that boat. It was good experience for me to make sure that our time on the water was constructive, and that we were all motivated. Our function was to try and push the A boat as hard as possible in the tuning and practice racing, so that they were as well primed as possible when it came to racing.

Certainly, the A boat were the better all-round team. And so they should have been. They had all the practice and preparation time. But we gave them some seriously tough races and did a really good job of pushing them hard. Every now and again it got a little bit heated. Grant would have to step in and calm things down. Both teams wanted to win so much. But that's the way it should have been. The other guys needed to be pushed. Whoever they raced against, they wouldn't get an easy ride.

However, the downside, from my perspective, was that my relationship with Dean was put under strain by the British press trying to wind the whole thing up. It wasn't really that way, especially from my point of view. But every time I did well in an event, or it was considered that Dean hadn't performed that well, they'd write about whether I'd come in and take his job.

As I've stressed, that wasn't the situation at all and I did my best to keep things defused. I wish now that Dean and I had had an honest chat about it. Instead we ended up being rather slightly stand-offish with each other. Fortunately, the rest of the team dealt with that situation really well. A few of the guys would use it as a good wind-up every now and then. The Kiwis are particularly ruthless when it comes to the art of ribbing someone, but it was all mostly good-natured.

I have a great affection for New Zealanders, even though they're terrible losers. The Aussies may hate the Brits, but the Kiwis, though they'd never admit it, have a much greater respect for Britain. They probably hold on tighter to their colonial links than Australians. Rugby, cricket and sailing, plus motorsports, are all big sports in New Zealand and it's amazing being down there. All the sailors are household names – which is not exactly the case in Britain. I would even get in a taxi, and the driver would ask me what I was doing, and what role I had in the team, and he'd say: 'Oh, you're Ben then, are you?'

There was a lot of tension at times. It could get a bit heavy. That was, in part, because of my own aspirations. I made it pretty clear that I wanted to helm an America's Cup boat one day. I never made any bones about that. I couldn't see why I shouldn't have been direct about what my ambitions were.

In fairness, I have to say that Grant Dalton was always supportive of that attitude. I liked Grant and we had a good relationship. He's a very direct guy and doesn't give a stuff about anything other than trying to win, so we got on quite well in that respect. I recognised that it may not have been my moment this time around. But he could see I wanted to achieve that in the future.

Basically I understood the deal to be this: Grant gave me the opportunity to learn, and be in a position to go on to helm and skipper a Cup boat in the future with the associated benefit for him that I pushed Dean. In a sense, it was like Dean having a very keen sparring partner in boxing.

If I'd have gone out and beaten Dean every day on the water then, yes, I'd have expected the job. But from where I'd come, with all the development and improvement required, that was never going to happen realistically. Dean is one of the very top guys out there.

Nevertheless, it was hugely frustrating, sitting on the coach boat and watching the guys on the A boat racing. But I had to take a very long-term view. I was learning from men like the afterguard coach, Rod Davis, I was with a top team, and racing against a top skipper like Dean.

The benefits would be confirmed in early 2009 when I skippered the TeamOrigin boat at a regatta in Auckland. It is something to which I will return, but my experience proved to be a great positive when we immediately plunged into the deep end and took on the likes of BMW Oracle Racing, Luna Rossa, Alinghi and, yes . . . Team New Zealand. Yet we were able to take on boats of that stature with not only a new team but one which had undergone little preparation. That was a real justification for all the time I'd spent as Dean's sparring partner ahead of the 2007 America's Cup. And, metaphorically, at least, getting beaten around the head.

Though I was unhappy about certain aspects of that period, I grew up so much in those two years. It was really frustrating at times, watching and wondering to myself what on earth was going on, but I learnt a lot that's really been good for me. I had to learn to stand up for myself and fight the battles that needed to be won.

Perhaps there was a feeling amongst some of the team that I was in it for personal glory. Most of that perception originated from my image. I was high profile purely because of the Olympics. So, whenever there was a story about Team New Zealand, inevitably it was distilled down to the basic components: me taking on Dean. In a way, the team didn't mind that supposed culture of conflict. It makes news. The sponsors like the coverage, so it helps commercially. That was something I was aware of from the beginning. However, in fact I worked really hard on being a team player and showing that I cared. That would have become clear from the moment we received the boats and began to prepare them for racing.

Team New Zealand did not have a massive budget, compared with BMW Oracle and Alinghi, whose boats would have been almost ready to sail when they received them.

In contrast, we were involved from an early stage of the boat's production, once it had come out of the mould. The sailing team were involved in sanding it down and applying non-stick material on the deck floor, that kind of thing. I remember I was in there at eight, nine, ten o'clock at night, sanding the inside of this boat with the other sailors. It was great from a team standpoint that we were all prepared to do that.

In the last six months we really got our act together when we started doing some serious team-building and development. There had been issues, about the guys being disaffected because they were on the B boat and not on the race boat. And then, all of a sudden, six months before we were due to race, someone brought the matter up and said: 'Why aren't we doing any of this team-building stuff? Here we are down in New Zealand and we're going to Valencia in two or three months, and then we'll soon go straight into the Louis Vuitton Cup. We need to be tight as a team, to be successful in what is a really long event; three or four months of racing, non-stop.'

We did some sessions with a guy named Robbie Deans, then the highly respected coach of the Auckland Crusaders, the top team in rugby league's Super 14. He came down and told us how they put a team together, how they worked well as a team, how they motivated people, and how they handled the issue of substitutes. A couple of weeks later it was rugby union's turn. The All Blacks coach Graham Henry came down and had a couple of sessions with us. In addition, some of the All Blacks came sailing. That was really enlightening.

Essentially, we set up our own team principles around the All Blacks' model, embracing core values, like trust and respect, which you need as a team, but which we'd never really spoken about. In fact, the whole lot of us, both the race team and the B team, went off to an island for a couple of days for team-building exercises. I'm not suggesting that we sat in a cave naked and chanted, or anything. But we did sit down and decide how we were going to attack this event as a team, and what was important to us.

We discussed what key areas we were going to work on: logistics, the boat set-up and preparation for the regatta, that kind of issue. Then we discussed the team and our core principles and values. We wrote down all those words which we thought were important. They included 'Respect'. 'Determination'. 'Courage'. 'Honesty'. We ended up with about twenty-five words that were crucial to the team, and being successful.

This may sound like a version of sports psychology. As I will discuss later, I'm not that keen on a team psychologist being involved with my own preparation for Olympic sailing. But this was not the same thing. This was the crew members themselves coming forward with important areas that would make us tight as a team and perform well – not an outside individual coming in and telling us what we should be doing, and thinking. Nor was it one of these business lectures, where they come up with loads of jargon and gobbledegook.

I was amazed with the results. It made a huge difference to us as a team. That wasn't necessarily one of our strengths beforehand. Probably we should have done it earlier.

Once our Cup boats had been manufactured and prepared down in New Zealand, we spent three or four months tuning them up as quickly as we could, and trained for what lay ahead. Physically and mentally, that was hard work, over long days. Training started at six in the morning. We used probably the best gym I've ever seen, Les Mills' World of Fitness. It actually opened at 5 a.m. As we were walking in, Grant Dalton would be walking out of it. He was in his early 50s, but a complete fitness freak. He always won the 'pull-up' test, or 'chins'. We all wound him up about his dubious technique, but because he was the boss we had to let him win!

At 7.30, it was down to the base for breakfast, and an eight o'clock meeting. Then it was getting the boats ready, packing and loading sails, and off the dock at 10.30. Then we'd be out on the water for five or six hours. Another meeting, and home for seven.

Finally, the boats were shipped to Valencia, where the 2007 America's Cup would be staged. In two months there, we continued tuning, through February and March. Then it was the final preparations, when we did a lot of in-house racing between the two boats. Meanwhile Dean and the A boat raced against some of the other teams to prepare for the Louis Vuitton Cup. That was the first major hurdle. All the twelve challenging teams contested that. The overall winner would go forward to take part in the America's Cup, against the holder, Alinghi.

The Louis Vuitton Cup is a round-robin series in which all the teams race each other, followed by quarter-finals and semi-finals. Team New Zealand raced the Spanish boat in the semis, and won easily. In the other semi, Luna Rossa beat BMW Oracle. Our boat raced Luna Rossa in the final of the Louis Vuitton Cup, and won through to race Alinghi for the America's Cup.

I can hear some people commenting that it's an unusual event in which the defending 'champions' go straight into the final, but history dictates that system, and people are, generally, happy with it.

We'd actually raced Alinghi in the warm-up to the Cup. I disagreed with that strategy. As the defender, they can't race in the Louis Vuitton Cup, so have no real gauge on how well they're progressing. But as one of the top teams, we gave them an accurate form guide.

We may have been many thousands of miles from our home base at Auckland, but there was tremendous New Zealand support in Valencia. From the docking area – the equivalent of Formula 1 garages – boats negotiate a canal to reach the sea. Every day, as we towed out both boats to tune up we'd pass an area of the harbour called 'Kiwi corner' where all their fans lined up. The noise and the atmosphere were phenomenal for a sailing event. There were also a lot of Swiss supporters, but they were outnumbered by the Kiwis.

Interestingly, though Alinghi are owned by Ernesto Bertarelli, the Swiss billionaire, their personnel otherwise consisted of 130 people from twenty-one other nations. Many, ironically enough, were Kiwis.

It was said that by the finale a football-size crowd of 75,000 spectators had assembled on shore for what turned out to be one of the closest contests in the event's history as Alinghi successfully defended their crown. It was really hard for everyone at Emirates Team New Zealand because the team had performed so well.

It was one of the most frustrating things I've done, sitting on the sidelines watching all the other teams racing, but it was what I had signed up to and I had to bite my lip and see it out. I was there, not racing, but having to be available, in case anything happened to Dean. We'd go out in the B boat to help tune up the race boat and then rush back to shore to watch the racing on TV where we had a better perspective.

To lose the Cup by such a small margin was incredibly tough on the whole team. I was disappointed but I hadn't been racing so it was more a disappointment for Dean and the guys. They were all completely shattered. They had been racing on and off for two months and to end it like that was terrible. As I've said, the Kiwis hate losing. That's probably why they are so successful in sport. I really felt for the guys, many of whom had become good mates, but I had to very quickly move on and turn my attention to the Finn and the 2008 Olympics.

My challenge for gold in 2008 had always been in the back of my mind. In 2006, I'd done the pre-Olympic test regatta at the sailing venue in Qingdao, and won that quite convincingly. It was the only race I did that year. In 2007, I missed the world championships in Cascais because they clashed with the America's Cup final. But I was keeping a close eye on how the other British sailors fared. Ed Wright was the highest finisher, in sixth place.

Immediately after the Cup finished, I had to go back to the UK. Then go straight out to Qingdao to do the pre-Olympic regatta. I had been really concerned that I'd left it late to pick up the Olympic side of things. It was a big risk, in truth.

Chapter 14

Battle to Qualify for Beijing

Those months preparing for the America's Cup were psychologically demanding. The tensions initially, and then watching as the team came so close to victory, brought a welter of conflicting emotions.

As I sat around watching the America's Cup in progress, knowing by now that, in reality, my work with the team was done, I knew there were guys training for, and competing in, the 2007 world championships in the Finn, including Brits.

I must confess there were times during those America's Cup exploits when I questioned whether I would be sufficiently prepared for Beijing. There was also a part of me that did wonder at one stage whether I wanted to make the transition back.

Yet, if there was one instant that persuaded me I wanted to continue as an Olympian, it was that special moment for all of us with British sport at heart, on 6 July 2005, that did it.

I'd been involved in the launch for the 2012 bid as an ambassador, and was at Trafalgar Square for the announcement by IOC president Jacques Rogge, in Singapore, that 'The Games of the XXXth Olympiad in 2012 are awarded to the city of . . . London.' It still sends tingles down my spine. The atmosphere was electric. It was a real motivator for me; a real inspiration.

I remember thinking at that instant: 'I've really got to be part of this. It's going to be amazing to have the Olympics here.' That was really the spark to become more heavily involved with Beijing and get my Olympic career back on track.

Although I'd been away, I kept my hand in. I'd won the worlds and European championships in 2005. The following year, I went down to Qingdao, venue for the sailing at the Beijing Games, to see what it was all about.

Qingdao is a coastal city that lies on the southern tip of China's Shandong Peninsula, and is located on Jiaozhou Bay, facing the Yellow Sea. It is a well-known holiday resort in China. But I knew the next few months would be no vacation for me.

As I've mentioned, I did the Olympic test regatta that year, and won. I hadn't sailed the Finn for a year, but enjoyed the challenging conditions: light winds and strong currents. It was a difficult venue. At one time I was quoted as saying that it was 'a sailor's nightmare'.

What I actually said, in an interview in the *Daily Telegraph*, was this: 'The evidence points to predominantly light winds with maybe one day of very strong winds. There are also interesting tides and conditions will be testing – some would say nightmarish. We need to stay patient. Get becalmed at the wrong time and you will drop ten places at the flick of a finger. All of us run the chance of having a very bad day, but Athens has taught me that you can recover.'

Strange though it may sound, such conditions were actually a boost for me. It would reward the more experienced sailors, such as myself. I don't think it's a coincidence that I came back in August, 2007, and won the pre-Olympic test regatta that year too.

Following that latter event I returned to full-time training in the Finn again. I went down to Australia in November to train there in earnest.

Despite those victories in the pre-Olympic test regattas, I didn't really expect to just walk back into the GB team as the Finn representative. While, for me, the Olympics had been in the background, one of my British rivals had only selection for the Games on his mind. Ed Wright, then ranked number five in the world, was concentrating on the event, and doing well. He won the European championships in 2006. It ensured it would be a difficult time for the selectors.

The main trial event had been the 2007 world championships at Cascais in Portugal, where Ed Wright had finished sixth. I was absent as it had clashed with the America's Cup. Though that had obviously been my own choice, I had won those two test events at Qingdao.

The RYA's Olympic Selection Committee named most of the sailors they wanted to represent Great Britain in October 2007. But the Finn class was one of the few where the nominations were postponed to allow for further trials. I was surprised by some of the attitudes towards me and the question of Olympic qualification, which was played out to a strange background.

Yes, I'd been away from single-handed sailing for some time to concentrate on the America's Cup. But I'd won the Finn world championships in 2005. And despite the fact that I'd basically sailed for only two weeks in the Finn before racing in the test regatta at Qingdao in 2006, I won by a long way. I'd repeated the feat in 2007, again quite comfortably, and without any practice. In neither case had I gone back to full-time training for it.

I guess that certain people just didn't like the idea of me 'swanning back', as they saw it, as GB's Finn representative, particularly as another Olympic gold medallist, Shirley Robertson, who was desperate to make Olympic history by becoming the first British woman to win three gold medals, had failed to make the GB team for Beijing.

The RYA had selected two of her Athens crew-mates, Sarah Ayton and Sarah Webb, together with Pippa Wilson, to contest the Yngling class after they took the world title in Cascais and won the final Olympic test event in China.

Shirley, who had taken time off and given birth to twins, had asked the RYA for an extension of the trials, but it was not forthcoming. Though I had dropped to 104th in the world rankings – for obvious reasons – I was more fortunate.

Admittedly, it was always going to be a difficult time for the selectors. I had been away concentrating on the America's Cup, although I'd kept my hand in. Ed Wright was focussing purely on the Finn, and doing quite well. Ultimately, the RYA attempted to be as fair as possible, which I think they were.

They decided that the Sydney International Regatta in December would be the main event of the selection trials which would lead to qualification for the Olympics. If it was still not possible after that for the selectors to make a decision, there were always the world championships at the end of January in Melbourne. I was philosophical about it. If I had to go out and prove myself, so be it.

So, it was back to the scene of my first Olympic triumph

seven years before in Sydney Harbour to ensure I made it to the start line, knowing that if I could could win decisively, the one available Olympic spot in the Finn would be mine.

It hadn't been the first time Ed or I had been involved in winner-takes-all qualification events. Four years previously, Ed, against whom I'd raced regularly since we had been teenagers in the youth squad, narrowly missed out on the Athens Olympics in the Laser class after losing out to Paul Goodison. Conversely, it will be recalled, I qualified for those Games by winning the world championships the year before, at the expense of my good friend 'Bart' Simpson, who finished third. It's exceptionally tough for those guys who don't qualify because of all the huge amount of time and effort they've put in. That's it; there's no consolation prize.

I thought back to when I was 19, and missed out on a gold at Atlanta, and thought 'Am I ever going to get the chance again . . .?' I knew how hard it can be to get selected, especially in the UK where we have so much strength and depth in all the classes every time.

Nevertheless I did find some of Ed Wright's comments to the media in the prelude to that Sydney event more than a little irritating. 'Ben's been away doing the America's Cup and, to be quite honest, he's not really sailing as well as he has done,' he told the *Independent on Sunday*. 'It's not a dissimilar situation to Shirley [Robertson]. She went off and did other things with her life for a while and gave that little chance to the other girls, and they stole it away from her. That's the way it is. This is such a high level in the sport that you can't just go away and expect to jump straight back in. What happened to Shirley does make me more confident.'

Ed's comments only served to fire me up even more. If there

was a hint of gamesmanship in his dealing with the press then it was severely misjudged and backfired spectacularly.

It wasn't the first time I'd had that kind of difficult situation. You will always have those rivalries. It's what spurs you on to train harder. In one way, what he said was good, because it really fired me up to go out and show that I hadn't lost it. In the Sydney International Regatta, I won six out of the eight races, which settled any argument. Ed didn't have his best event, finishing fifth, and I got the selection.

I couldn't feel sorry for him. My job's to go out there and try and win races. That's competition. He's a great sailor, but we've got such depth of talent. It's just a shame we can't have more than one representative in each class.

From Ed's point of view, I'm sure it was very disappointing for him, and difficult to accept. In fairness, afterwards he was really good about it; very grown up. You can only respect someone for taking it that way rather than going off in a huff and sulking. He got back into it, and sailed pretty well at the 2008 world championships where I won and he was seventh. He was keen to keep going to 2012, which was a positive way to deal with it.

Disappointment, if you allow it, can be a terribly negative, destructive influence. From my early days, I have used dis-appointment as a fuel to work harder, improve on what went wrong and not let it happen again. It will no doubt have become apparent by now that I'm a terrible loser. I hate it. I'm better than I used to be, but it still hurts like hell. It's the biggest motivator there is.

It's why I try to minimise that by leaving nothing to chance in the build-up to a major regatta like an Olympics or world championships.

Physical preparation is vitally important. Typically, I'll go and do an aerobics session before or just after breakfast. Then there's boat maintenance, followed by sailing for three to five hours. By the I time I pack the boat up, it'll be four or five o'clock. I'll do weight sessions in the gym in the evening. It's a full-on day. Not like some sports where you can do a couple of hours in the morning, and that's it.

You can't fully replicate on land the demands of sailing in a major event. But by the time of an Olympics or world championships, you need to feel that you're at your peak, and your body can withstand the rigours to come.

There will always be some weight training, but what I do in the gym depends on the sailing venue, and what the winds are like. Whether I'm trying to increase or decrease my muscle mass, maintain it, or get stronger, or maybe work more on the aerobic side of things, a lot of science goes into it.

We have a strength and conditioning coach, Steve Gent, who puts together a weights programme, depending on conditions. Steve's a member of the England Institute of Sport team. He works alongside the RYA's senior sports science officer, Pete Cunningham, to ensure the strength and conditioning training the sailors are doing is sailing-specific. It's great working with those guys.

Strangely enough, I do enjoy it, especially once I get in a routine. And that's a word that becomes very important as the Games approach.

Getting the details right is important at an Olympics. Even accommodation and food. At Qingdao, the GB team stayed in a hotel rather than the athletes' accommodation provided. We'd been there the two years previously, and had got to know the hotel staff very well. It was like going home to a family. They were incredibly sweet, and hard-working and caring. We even had our own chef. If that sounds somewhat indulgent, the problem with that was that, while eighty per cent of the team were trying to lose weight, and were happy to have tiny portions of rice with boiled chicken and steamed broccoli, that kind of thing, I was trying to maintain mine.

Everybody else's food was zero fat. I needed something with more substance to it, as did Bart and Iain. For them, in the Star, like me, weight wasn't so much an issue. We snuck out to the Italian, or one of the other western-style restaurants in town – there was one particular buffet available at the Shangri-la Hotel that was a great favourite.

Certainly, once it gets to race days, I am very much a creature of routine. I get up at the same time, have a good warm-up and stretch, followed by breakfast.

I get down to the boat well before the race, and always clean the bottom of it; make sure it's spotless. No, it's not obsessive-compulsive disorder! For me, it's just being professional. There could be grease on the boat, anything.

I always leave the beach, or dock, at the same time before the race. I always do the same pre-start routine. I make sure I tick off all the boxes. Then I'm confident I can get on and race. If I didn't I'd feel unsettled. That is all as important as being fit and tactically prepared.

What irritates me most about competing is returning after a race, and hearing someone say: 'Oh, I was winning. But then there was a big wind-shift,' or 'There was something on the bottom of my boat.' Well, that's just nonsense. Just excuses. It's really irritating. In fact, by inference, it's insulting to the man who *is* performing well. Because these are generally con-trollables. It's totally down to you. If something breaks on the boat, unless you're really unfortunate, it's normally because you haven't checked something.

That's why one of my maxims, if you like, is: No Excuses.

Mind you, for a time in the summer of 2008, it did look as though a freak event could give us all an excuse for not racing at all.

A couple of months before the Games, sailing suddenly received an inordinate amount of coverage, even in the 'popular' media. The reason? As *The Times* headline put it: *Mutant seaweed may sink sailing hopes at Beijing Olympics*. We were informed by Ashling O'Connor, their Olympics correspondent, that 'They have battled dense smog, strong tides and no wind but now British sailors training for the Beijing Games are contending with mutant seaweed that has invaded the Olympic venue in China. The bright green algae, described as "thick as a carpet", is making it impossible for dinghies to navigate the course that will host the Olympic regattas in less than two months.' It was 'wrapping itself around keels, bringing the boats to a standstill.'

The 'seaweed' was believed to have drifted in from the Yellow Sea following recent bad weather. Local fishermen were trying to clear the area, armed only with their nets slung over the side of their small boats. Iain Percy was quoted as saying it was 'a real concern'. Clearly it was for the BOA, too, with sailing being one of Britain's strongest events, with nine medal hopes.

I was fortunate. I only heard on the news how bad it was. I'd done a three-week stint at Qingdao in May, and it was just as I and my training partners left that the 'seaweed' came in. For people training there in June, it was a major issue. It seriously affected their training. It's no fun trying to sail through miles and miles of green algae and not getting anywhere. The Chinese worked really hard to clear it up and when we returned in July it had pretty much disappeared.

The training preparation went really well and I was very fortunate to have five great training partners out in China. Ed Wright was already looking towards 2012 and it was great of him to come out and train along with the up-and-coming youth world champion Giles Scott. Andrew Mills, Ed Greg and Mark Andrews, also younger talented sailors, came out and so at all times we had five boats on the water and could hold small-scale races on the Olympic racetrack. It's great to have new talent coming into the sport and personally I get a big motivation training with these guys as they're so enthusiastic and are really into their fitness.

People assume that we always sail in some wonderful pristine environment. It's not always the case. Sydney Harbour, of course, has its ferries. But undoubtedly the filthiest waters I've ever encountered were in Rio Harbour, which is festooned with loads of rubbish, the result of massive tidal rips. You encounter it all: pieces of furniture, oil drums, dead cats, all floating around.

That said, I think we can be pretty confident of 2012 and the sailing venue of Weymouth in the summer of that year. The weather could be anything, but I can vouch for the fact that it is an excellent sailing location, providing a good and fair test.

But back to Qingdao. I was aware that by the time I had reached the sailing venue I was more than just a strong favourite. According to some in the media and, I believe, the bookmakers, who had made me well odds-on, I just had to turn up and, a week later, collect my medal.

You must always have a massive respect for the opposition. I knew that, in these light, difficult conditions, there were four or five guys, like myself, who had been in the class for a good period of time, and would make their experience count. The Spaniard Rafa Trujillo had won the silver at Athens; the Dane, Jonas Christensen had won the world championships in 2006; the Greek Emilios Papathanasiou had been in the world top three for four years. He was really good in the light airs, also.

There were also new, younger faces coming through who were pushing really hard and presented a threat: the Croatian representative, Ivan Kljakovic; the American, Zach Railey; Dutchman Pieter-Jan Postma. Also my old French adversary, Guillaume Florent, was back for another shot at the title.

Including myself, there were about ten of us who had the ability to win a medal in Qingdao. On their day, if they sailed really well, and, just as crucially, you didn't get it right, they could beat you. It really was very open.

That's why I knew I must be one hundred per cent prepared, and do everything properly, in terms of the equipment and getting my fitness honed. That was the only way I was going to win that event. Not by just turning up and cruising.

Chapter 15

Sickness Doesn't Deter Me

Despite all your best-laid plans, sometimes you are struck down by something utterly beyond your control. Three days before the start of the Beijing Games, I wondered if I'd even get to the start line.

The immediate build-up to the Olympics hadn't gone brilliantly for me. There were a few niggles. First the media interest. You expect a lot of attention in the weeks leading up to any Olympics; but, at a certain point, you try to switch to competition mode. It's a difficult one, because you have a responsibility to talk to the press. But at the same time, all you're interested in is competing and staying focussed. I think as a team we could have done a better job of cutting out any distractions in the final three to four days before racing started.

Also, a few days before the start of the Games, the GB sailing team flew to a holding camp in Shanghai, about 1,000 kilometres away from Qingdao. There some time for a little R&R, meetings about rules, the logistics of our events, and there was some team-building, with some motivational speeches from the team psychologist, Ben Chell.

His message was pretty basic stuff about having the

confidence to succeed, but he was really trying to build us all up, as a group. I guess it was valuable to some of the younger members of the team, but it was really the wrong message for me personally. When it comes to psychology, we're all different and I didn't need that. To my mind, it's all about getting my own preparation right.

At a big event like an Olympics, I'm highly focussed. I just concentrate on getting my head down and immersing myself in my own performance – so much so that, to some people, I possibly come across as being too self-centred, although that's not the case.

There were certain team issues I wasn't altogether happy with in terms of the way that things were set up. But I tried not to make too much of an issue out of it. As long as they didn't impact too heavily on my preparations there was no point in creating a massive amount of friction by voicing my opinion on how things should be run. Doing that quickly snowballs, and doesn't necessarily help you or the team in the long term.

As a competitor, I try not to get involved in the political side of the sport. But maybe when I've retired from Olympic sailing, who knows? I often feel guilty that I haven't put more back into sailing because I've been so busy racing. I'd like to help with the future development of the sport.

Certainly from a youth perspective, I think that these days there is far too much pressure put on kids to compete at certain events and train in a certain way. It's no surprise that we lose many of them when they reach burnout far too early. The focus must be on logistical support, financial support and coaching. Not trying to predetermine someone's life from the age of 12. If a young person is truly determined to make it, then they will normally get there but they need to be allowed to make their own mistakes and learn from them. Anyway, in the future I hope I can help and put a little bit back.

At Qingdao, I worked closely with Jez Fanstone, my coach. Lymington-based, he used to sail Finns when he was younger, and then became a professional sailor. He did a couple of Whitbread races; one with Lawrie Smith on *Silk Cut*, back in 1994, and skippered *News Corp*, sponsored by Rupert Murdoch, in 1998. He had become involved with the RYA after Athens, and after 2006, came on board as the Finn coach. He's a really good guy, and once I qualified in 2008, we worked very closely the whole way through.

My own pre-race preparation is all about getting my mind in gear. I have a pre-race plan, and if I haven't ticked off all the key areas, both physically within myself, and technically, with the boat, I don't feel comfortable. I can't perform to my optimum. Psychologically, that's vital. It's about leaving nothing to chance. Going through the whole programme, seeing where the weaknesses are, and eliminating as many of them as you can.

When you actually reach the start, you change mode. You say to yourself, 'Right, this is it. Switch on.' You sweep everything that's not to do with the race out of your mind. You must be one hundred per cent attuned to everything that is important within the race. In a way, that happens subconsciously, anyway, but I try to trigger that.

An Olympic race lasts for anything between an hour and two hours. It's you against the conditions and the opposition for roughly the duration of a football match. And there's no half-time managerial pep talk for us.

Of course, we all can be easily sidetracked. But one of my strengths, a factor which always gives me confidence, is that once I start racing, I find I very rarely get distracted. Even when

I've been racing and maybe things have not been going that well on a personal level, I've always been pretty good at dealing with that and not letting it affect my performance.

Off the water, I worry about things as much as the next person. Things can prey on my mind if I'm not happy about something. But when I go racing, I'm very good at switching off from those issues. It's amazing how the mind can do it. Once racing has finished, then you revert to your normal self, with the same weaknesses as everyone else.

As it was, the scheduling of that holding camp in Shanghai only just about gave me enough time to get back to Qingdao, and get properly prepared for my event, so it wasn't ideal. But worse was to follow.

The morning we set out to fly back from Shanghai to Qingdao, I woke to find my face was a little swollen. Although it didn't appear to be anything major, I was concerned. We arrived back at Qingdao and I had an early night. I got up in the morning to discover that my condition had worsened. My face had become swollen horribly on both sides, although more so on the right. It was weird looking at myself in the mirror. 'Shit,' I thought, 'what's happening? I look like the Elephant Man.' This, I should stress, was three days before the start of my event, and could really have been an issue.

I called David Gorrod, the team doctor, who diagnosed it as mumps, which was a relief, of sorts. It is a viral disease, which tends to affect the salivary glands in the cheeks, and though it is most common in children, can be caught by older people. The immediate problem was that, in the first few days, it is contagious. We had to ensure that I did not pass it on to anyone else in the team, so I had to go into isolation. I had to eat on my own, and avoid contact with the rest of my teammates when I

Reacting to another bad Kiwi wind-up during training

The legendary bowman Joey Allen talking me through a pre-start

The 3km running test, not my favourite pastime

Dean Barker and I looking serious in Valencia

It was a huge honour to be announced as helmsman for TeamOrigin in September 2007

(*Facing page*) A steep learning curve: being talked through the match-racing game by one of the best, Rod Davis

(*Left*) Celebrating finishing the JP Morgan Asset Management Round the Island race aboard Alex Thomson's *Hugo Boss*, with Lewis Hamilton as special guest.
(*Below*) The last race in Beijing, winning gold in awesome conditions for sailing

(*Left*) Victory in the rain after receiving my third gold, from Princess Anne (*Above*) Celebrating with friends. Iain's and Bart's Star gold was a great way to end a brilliant team performance in China

Showing on-water aggression during qualification for Beijing

Taking the JP Morgan Asset Management Extreme 40 under Tower Bridge after the Beijing Games

Meeting the Queen with fellow gold medallists at Buckingham Palace after China. I am with Andrew Simpson, Iain Percy, Pippa Wilson and Sarah Gosling

Sir Richard Branson's boat setting off
on the Transatlantic record attempt
(*Above*) Good times during the attempt
with Mike Sanderson and Sir Richard

(*Above*) Racing Coutts and co. in Auckland

(*Right*) Racing during the LV Cup in
Auckland with TeamOrigin

(*Left*) Winning the German match tour with
TeamOrigin guys Iain Percy, Christian
Kamp, Mike Mottl and Matt Cornwell

was down at the dinghy park. They all thought it was hilarious, of course. Just the sight of my puffed-out cheeks prompted them to start calling me 'Alvin', like the character in *Alvin and the Chipmunks*, the eighties' TV series. I suppose it was quite amusing.

It wasn't the first time I'd suffered from illness during my career. As I have mentioned before, I was stricken with glandular fever early in 2004. I was really quite sick, and things were really tough through to May the following year. That was a period in which I was trying to race and build up to the world championships in Rio in January, then the European champion-ships, and also prepare for the Athens Olympics. I still suffer from it now if I push myself too hard or get run down. If I do get a relapse, I'm out of order for about a week. Obviously, it affects my preparations.

I had felt good this time in the build-up to the Games. Now, three days before I started racing, I didn't need this. But make no mistake; I was going to get through it and race whatever. After all, it wasn't like a broken arm or something. I admit, though, that I was worried. I knew that this condition could affect my chances of gold. There's no remedy, other than time. You just have to get over it. David Gorrod advised me to spend the day in bed. 'I don't want you pushing yourself,' he said.

Pretty ironic, when you consider that in a couple of days' time I would have to 'push myself' to the ultimate . . .

Frankly, I was really wondering if I was going to make it. You're almost laughing at the timing. It couldn't have come at a worse time. But you have to deal with it in the best possible way, and carry on as though nothing has happened. I also had to keep it quiet. It would probably have been quite a big story if it had got out. Fortunately, it didn't – despite the fact that being in isolation meant I had to use the hotel restaurant where many of the sailing journalists were staying, which was pretty comical!

The following day, I was able to take part in a practice race. That was important because I didn't want my rivals becoming wise to my condition. It could have been damaging when all my preparation had been designed to convince my opponents that they were fighting for silver. If that sounds a bit arrogant, let me say this: I've always tried to let my sailing and my results do the talking. I'm not one for trying to play mind games or 'bigging myself up' in interviews.

I had not competed much since Athens – but had contested the world and European championships and a regatta in Palma in 2008, and won them all. That was important to me. While the results were close, it perhaps gave me a psychological advantage in that I had not been beaten in the four years since Athens.

The consequence, as I've said already, was everyone was declaring that I just had to turn up to secure a third Olympic gold medal in successive Games.

I didn't mind that. Ultimately, I'd rather be the favourite than not. It was something I expected because of my record in the class. I'd won gold at Athens, and five world championships in the Finn. People were also aware that this was a venue that rewarded experience. So, the talk was inevitable.

Except it doesn't work like that. It was ridiculous really; especially at a venue where conditions were so capricious. I knew it was going to be really hard to win. The wind and the tide were always of concern. That was why I spent as much time as possible training there. I also put a lot of effort into sail development for that venue.

Racing's never as straightforward as people outside the sport imagine. There's an appearance that it's easy for me because of the results I'd had. It looks like I'm streets ahead. But it's not like that all. People don't realise how close these other guys are in ability. It's the same in most sports at the elite level. Remember, everyone assumed, ahead of Sydney, that Steve Redgrave would win his final race, to secure his fifth gold. Steve managed it, but he won by what? A few millimetres. It's nothing at the end of two kilometres. The same with Matthew Pinsent at the Athens Games, when he claimed his fourth gold.

I knew what a difficult task lay ahead. And I was also aware that, by fair means or otherwise, nobody was going to make things easy for me. The thing about the Olympics is that everyone's demeanour changes massively.

Suddenly no one is your mate any more. The slightest little infringement of the rules on the water and someone's going to try and nail you with a protest. There's lots of little psychological wind-ups going on. I knew the other guys were targeting me. They saw that as the only way they were going to beat me, through the protest room, claiming rule infringements, to try and get a cheap disqualification.

The first couple of days were the worst. Anyone I went near, I had to be ultra-cautious. It was clear again that a lot of the guys were intent on giving me a hard time. And so it proved. On the second day, in the first race, I crossed in front of the American Zach Railey. It was a fair manoeuvre and I avoided tacking across in front of him and fouling him. But he went round the mark and shouted 'I could have hit you. I'm going to protest.' I shouted back: 'What are you talking about? I was never going to foul you and, in fact, I crossed you and let you go in front of me.' He said: 'No, no. This is the Olympics; I'm protesting.'

In those circumstances you do two full penalty turns. I could have got angry and ignored him, but though it may sound ridiculous, you have to be pragmatic. It exonerates you from any further disciplinary action, so that's what I did. It felt like he was playing a card but I played it safe. It will be recalled from that incident involving the Frenchman, Guillaume Florent, in Athens that if you do nothing and it ends up in the protest room the onus is on you to prove to the jury that nothing happened, with the possibility of disqualification. Better to lose a placing, or two, than that. Sailing is a real mental game. Some make an analogy with chess, and that's very true. You've got to think ahead about every move you and your opponents might make.

Yes, it was really annoying, but I drew on my experience. I used it in the right way to not get too wound up. I put my frustration back into the sailing. I had to be conservative. It cost me a few places earlier on in the regatta, but it prevented me getting a cheap disqualification. It was really hard. Part of me wanted to lose my temper and get stuck into him; to try to take him out in the next race. But I knew that I couldn't get involved in those little games.

Meanwhile I was still worried about how my illness was affecting me. My event started on the first Saturday of the Games and, in fact, I was fine for the first two days. But as I got into the week, I became increasingly tired. There were a couple of days when we were hanging around in the intense heat, waiting to race because there was no wind, and I was really struggling. I felt low and lacked energy. Though sailing is what the Aussies mockingly call one of the 'sitting down' sports at which the British excel, it requires an incredible amount of fitness. Fortunately, though I felt rough, it never got so bad that I felt it was impeding my performance. I can only think that the adrenalin of racing got my body through it, to some extent.

The wind at the beginning of the week was really light and

patchy which can result in quirky scores. For example, in the first race of the series, I was well in the lead, then, down the last leg, the wind turned inside out and I went from first to tenth. That was crazy and seriously frustrating. But it was always going to be like that at that venue, the way that the wind and currents were. But because I was aware of that, it became a positive thing for me rather than a negative. My experience meant I was able to deal with it, and not get flustered. I went out and won the next race, and built a series from then on in.

After that first race my results, with one exception, were consistently good. By the end of Monday, after six of the nine races, I was the overall leader; a position I maintained until the penultimate day, Friday. On the Saturday, the medal race was scheduled to take place. That carries double points. I would go into that twelve points ahead of my nearest challenger, Zach Railey, the American. It meant I didn't have to win. I just had to finish within six places of him.

By then I felt really good, both competitively and health-wise, even though the race was postponed for twenty-four hours, until the Sunday, because of the light wind.

The following morning – having 'fuelled up' on a double portion of lasagne the evening before – I looked out of my window to see grey clouds. As one writer said of me: 'These were his kind of conditions, a whiff of home.' In fact, they were the exact opposite to what we'd experienced earlier in the week: it was windy, with big waves. That's what I love. I could sail my own race. Not place my fortunes in the lap of the gods.

In these conditions, sailing is much more about boat-handling and fitness. I sailed out to the course early to prepare and watch 'The Yngling Girls' completely nail their medal race and win gold. I was impressed and it motivated me. But then the rain came down, the visibility was virtually nil, and we had to go back in again. It was incredibly frustrating.

I thought 'When are we ever going to do this race?' Finally, it cleared. Jez Fanstone, my coach, saw they'd dropped the postponement flag. He rushed over and said 'You're on.' His words were like music to the ears. I ran to the boat. In those conditions, I was very confident about my speed and my fitness was fine.

Chapter 16

Britain's Sailors on the Crest of a Wave

The gold was mine. Just as long I did nothing rash. In my impetuous youth that could have been the case; it was partly why I was denied gold by my deadly rival, the Brazilian Robert Scheidt, at Atlanta, as a wide-eyed 19-year-old in 1996, and had to settle for a silver medal in my first Games. Only one man could defeat me now, and that was the one whose reflection stared back at me from the water as I prepared to head out for the start of my final race at Qingdao.

But now, blessed with the experience which had brought me two subsequent Olympic golds, at Sydney and Athens, I was supremely confident. I was prepared and I knew precisely what I had to do. As I set out on that final race of my Olympic event at Qingdao, I kept saying to myself 'Just make sure you don't capsize,' or, as we are more likely to mutter when we're under pressure in sailing, 'Don't piss it in.'

All I had to do was make sure I got my boat down to the finish without blowing the whole thing. Surely, I couldn't do that.

Not after getting this far, after overcoming illness just before the start of the Games.

I enjoyed a great race in awesome conditions, established a good lead and never lost it. All that could thwart me now was the possibility of capsizing. Down the last downwind leg, I just repeated the words in my mind, like some religious chant: 'Must just get it across the finish line.' Normally I'd be pumping the sail very hard and really going for it. Instead I was just sitting there, trying to get home as safely as I could.

It's funny. I thought about my training partners who might have been watching the race on television, shaking their heads in disapproval at my poor technique. But it was safe; it didn't need to look good.

At the finish, I experienced a sense of relief followed by profound satisfaction at what I'd done. There was an outpouring of emotion with the realisation that I'd achieved something I'd been so focussed on for so long. This was, by far, my most exhilarating and exciting win. I was far more animated than I'd ever been before, more pumped up with that than I had been with any other event at any other Games because I was able to win the race, and win gold, in a fitting style.

In hindsight, Atlanta was a bit disappointing. As far as I knew then, that could have been my one and only tilt at an Olympic gold. At Sydney, I didn't know if I'd won or not because there was going to be a protest regardless of the race result. I certainly didn't start jumping around then, because it wasn't over.

Athens had been pretty anticlimactic because I just had to finish within fifteen points of the guy who was behind me in the overnight placings. That meant we both sailed conservatively. I just stuck with him and we finished the race in thirteenth and fifteenth places. In the end, I was hugely relieved to have won after the terrible start I'd had to the series.

Now, here at Qingdao, this was so much more rewarding and exciting because I'd had so much pressure. I'd had to deal with my illness, and there'd been so great a build-up to it all. I was not tearful, but I came close. It had been a huge test. People may think it could not compare with breasting the line first in, say, the 100m, but for me it was the ultimate experience. I sailed straight over to Jez to celebrate. He had put so much into the campaign and spent many months away from his family in New Zealand. I was as relieved for him that our plan had come together and the efforts were definitely worthwhile.

The first people I phoned were my parents. They were at home, in Cornwall, and had been watching events via the internet or television. My dad and my mother, and my sister, Fleur, have been there for me all the way. Many others, too. People sometimes forget the massive team who are behind our medals: coaches, sports physiologists, trainers, my business manager Jo, family and friends, sponsors. A massive effort goes into making it happen.

Dad had been so important to what I had achieved. A lot of fathers would probably have interfered when I was young, but he knew better. He gave me advice, but it was always uncomplicated and impartial. No matter what the situation is, if I'm in a boat, it's always my dad's voice that's there in the back of my head. 'Keep it simple,' I hear him say.

The media inevitably concentrated on my becoming Britain's most successful sailor. 'So now he has more medals than Rodney Pattison who won two golds and a silver in the Mexico City, Munich and Montreal Olympics,' it was said of me in the *Guardian*. I tried to put my feelings into words for the sports writers at the press conference which followed my victory: 'When I was a kid all of my generation looked up to him [Pattison]. We were in awe of what he achieved and it seems a little bit surreal to be in the position I am in now,' I said. 'It has been a long road but I have really enjoyed all of my Olympic sailing career whether it has been the Games or the journey along the way.'

I was asked if I considered myself 'Superman'.

I've never knowingly been one for hyperbole, so I replied: 'As far as I know I'm human.' It probably wasn't quite what the writers were hoping for. But to be honest, I prefer any analysis of my abilities to come from others.

Jacques Rogge wasn't able to present me with my medal. He sent me an email, apologising for that, with the words: 'From a humble Finn sailor to an Olympic star'. Later, the IOC president provoked some debate by declaring in an interview with the BBC that my achievement in winning a third sailing gold was the equal of Michael Phelps' or Usain Bolt's feats. The Jamaican sprinter had won gold in the 100m and 200m, winning both in world-record times, while the US swimmer had broken Mark Spitz's thirty-six-year-old record by winning eight gold medals in Beijing.

'For me, his achievement is as valid as Phelps or Bolt,' Rogge, who competed in the sailing in the 1968, 1972 and 1976 Games, said of my success. 'I don't like to compare athletes from different sports, but Ben Ainslie competes in a boat class where he can only win one medal. The others [Phelps and Bolt] can win two, three . . . all the way up to eight. What they do is fantastic, but what Ainslie does is equally fantastic.' As a former sailor himself, that was high praise.

Celebrations on the night of my triumph were relatively

modest. I went out with Jez, my coach, and we had a few beers but you try not to go crazy out of respect for the people still racing. Because the rest of the team were generally being so successful, the celebrations continued throughout the second week. But you also had to be mindful that there were also people who were really down about the way things had gone.

The next day I felt ropey from my illness and my exertions, although part of that was probably alcohol-induced. Just as with the after-effects of glandular fever, the adrenalin of racing gets your body through it, to some extent. Afterwards you have a bit of a collapse.

There was never any question of a dash for home after my event had ended. You are part of a team, and you don't just pack up your boat and leave, but encourage the other guys still competing. It is important that you go down to the dinghy park and try and cheer them on. It's the right thing to do, although I would be there, anyway. It was a massive plus that, at the last two Games, my event was in the first week.

What I don't do, though, is dispense advice.

As friends, Iain Percy and Bart Simpson, competing together in the double-handed keelboat class, and I, would always talk about how the racing was going. But just because of my own achievements I don't consider myself as possessing some kind of guru status. There are some characters in sailing who I feel are suited to giving advice and imposing themselves on people. But that's not me. I find that a little bit arrogant.

I've never wanted to come across as 'the great I am'. It's not my way. I've always felt, if someone wants to ask me for advice they'll come and ask. To be honest, not many people have. At that level, all members of the GB team are very good sailors. They know what they're doing. Having said that, I have sometimes wondered whether I've appeared to be stand-offish to other people in the team. Maybe they felt that that they couldn't come and ask. I hope not. But it's a fine balance.

Of course, cheering on your GB teammates is a lot more easily done if you've got a medal. The hardest thing is if somebody's racing in the first week and had a really lousy event. That's when it's difficult. If they're in a really negative mindset, do they really want to be there, and should they be if, understandably, all they want to do is disappear and get home to their family?

As for myself, in the second week I'd have a good lie-in, wander down to the venue as the sailors were launching their boats, watch the racing, and then tried to be around when they arrived back. If someone had won a medal, I'd maybe go and have a beer with them in the evening to celebrate their success.

I had to raise many a glass. It was phenomenal coming down every morning, and at the end of each day, there'd be another British sailor winning a medal. Though we got talked up a lot as a team beforehand, we surprised ourselves. We had prepared very well, and we had a really good sailor in each class.

In the final medal table, Britain came fourth with nineteen golds, thirteen silver, and fifteen bronze; a total of forty-seven. Better even than sixth-placed Australia. Of those, sailing contributed four golds and six medals overall. However, it must be remembered that, compared with, say, cycling, sailors can only contest one event. In context, it was a brilliant effort all round.

People rated Paul Goodison as a favourite going into the Games, as I had, but also knowing the Laser class and how fickle it can be, I knew it would be hard for Paul. Actually 'Our Kid' made it look easy, winning comfortably, which was great to watch because he's a really good mate of mine – as, of course, are Iain Percy and Bart Simpson. The Star always looked like it was going to be a really open event. I thought they'd get a medal, it was just a question of which one.

I had watched Iain, who was then sailing with Steve Mitchell, lose out on a medal in Athens and that was hard to deal with and as a friend very hard to offer consolation. Thankfully, this time around, sailing with Bart, it was a different story.

After I had crossed the finish line, and won my gold, and could relax, I was asked to commentate on Bart's and Iain's final race for the BBC. I initially declined, but Richard Simmonds, who was commentating for the BBC and has become a good friend over the years, talked me into it. The Star medal race was such a close affair. It's terrible watching. You're so nervous, but there's nothing you can do. You're mentally screaming at them: 'What are you doing!?'

Starting in the silver position, the important thing was that they beat the overnight leaders, Sweden. They did, and though the boys actually finished fifth, it was enough to claim the gold. For me, it was one of the best sporting moments I had ever witnessed. It sounds strange to say it, but I was even more emotional about that result than my own. Here were my two best friends, guys who had sailed with and against each other since the age of 7, putting a fine performance together.

I knew how much it meant to Bart, competing in his first Olympics and described by our Olympic manager Stephen Park as 'the nearly man'. He'd just missed out on the Olympics before. In 2000, Iain had beat him to Finn qualification, and in 2004 I had done so. It was also a special moment for Iain. He'd won gold in 2000, then had a really tough time of it in 2004 when he and Steve Mitchell finished sixth in the Star. After that, he had had paired up with Bart in the same class, but things had not gone their way. They'd had quite a tough year leading up to Beijing, and put all their effort into developing a new boat. It meant they hadn't really focussed on the racing. Everyone had tended to write them off. But in fact the new boat made a big difference, and they were able to go out and win. Runners–up, incidentally, were the Brazilian pair, one of whom was a certain Robert Scheidt.

When Iain and Bart arrived back at the dock they were exhausted, though that didn't stop us throwing them in the water, together with Stephen Park.

As for our other medal-winners, I thought the Yngling girls would win, as they did in fine style. I was sure that Nick Rogers and Joe Glanfield would get a medal in the men's 470, but wasn't sure which. It turned out to be a silver. Bryony Shaw was fantastic. She became the first British woman to win an Olympic windsurfing medal, with her bronze in the RS:X. I really felt for those who just missed out on a medal. Watching Nick Dempsey's medal race in the RS:X was excruciating. He went from gold to fourth in a race which was too short for the typically light Qingdao conditions.

We had a massive celebration on the last night. We all got pretty drunk, though perhaps we could be forgiven any excess. As always, after training incredibly hard for three or four months, and being away from home, all the emotions came out, and a few people's alter egos emerged. Let's just say, a few people got things off their chest which they had been holding in for a while.

What you have to remember is that with any Games, probably only about ten per cent of the people are happy with how they've done. Another group, say sixty, seventy per cent, are actually pretty pissed off with life. So, after the Games, not everyone is going to totally immerse themselves into the party atmosphere. There will be a lot of depressed people around; people wondering what they're going to do with their life. So, it's actually quite a weird environment.

The people who have done well are really happy for themselves and their team. But how do you react to those who haven't done so well? You don't want to be partying in someone's face, yelling, 'Isn't life wonderful?' You've got to be a bit sensitive. Even then, what do you say? 'Hard luck'? In such circumstances, I feel it was better to let them work through their disappointment themselves. There were a few people who hadn't done as well as they'd hoped, and it was really tough for them.

The 49er guys were such a case in point. Stevie Morrison and Ben Rhodes were really down, having been favourites to get a medal. They had a terrible event, and didn't get anywhere near it. Then they had to spend a whole week and watch everyone else win medals. I'm not sure I could have dealt with it as well as they did. I talked to them, but about everything except the sailing. Just everyday things. Their girlfriends had arrived, so we chatted about where they'd be going with them.

You felt desperately sorry for them. You knew how much effort they'd put into it. But they're great sailors and I'm sure they'll do well in the future.

It had been bad enough for me in Atlanta, just missing out on the gold. I thought back to that day, twelve years earlier, when I had wondered if that was it: that my Olympic career was over. It is so hard to win selection; especially in Britain where we have so much strength and depth in all the classes. It will be difficult for me in 2012. I take nothing for granted. Giles Scott, the world junior champion in the Finn, is highly promising, and could come through in time for the Olympics. And, no doubt, Ed Wright will be poised for qualification again.

Much had been made beforehand of the decision to award Beijing the Games. Looking back, I think it was a good thing overall for them to be staged there. It opened that nation up. Whatever its reason for bidding for the Games, it had the effect of bringing the spotlight on it: politically, in terms of human-rights issues, its rate of industrialisation, and its pollution. But when all is said and done, it was still a fantastic Olympics. What they put into the infrastructure was way beyond anything else we've ever seen.

Admittedly, sailing-wise, well, it wasn't the greatest event in terms of conditions or water. In fact, it was pretty lousy. But as sailors we had to accept that was the way it was. We knew how it would be from as long as six years out, and embrace that. And let's be honest: Sydney, for all its attributes, is not necessarily the best sailing test in the world, as I discovered on my first visit. But you have to deal with what is in front of you. You have to make it work.

From my brief view of China, there are many things to like about the country. I'm not sure if they slip happy pills into their drinks every morning, but the people always appeared content with life. They were certainly delighted that the Olympics were there, and that we were there. They were massive fans of the Olympics and the sailing, and put a huge amount of effort into ensuring that everything ran smoothly for us.

However, the standard of living for some was seriously low, as you observed if you drove round some of the slum areas in the backstreets. Obviously, they don't have a great welfare system.

Before the Games, I was asked by journalists about the

protests in cities, including London, objecting to China hosting the Olympics. It would be naive to think that these Games weren't overshadowed by political issues. I could understand that people may well have pertinent objections, regarding China's policy towards Tibet, for example.

The Chinese, IOC and BOA dealt with it all reasonably well. We had some strong advice from the BOA in terms of dealing with political issues. We were firmly instructed not to get on to areas like Darfur, Tibet and human-rights issues in interviews. To be honest, though you know some of the background of the country, you don't know enough to have a view on it, anyway. I didn't want to get involved in politics. My concern was that the Olympics would become hijacked, and have their success threatened, so that certain people could push their point across.

Normally I'd say that if sportspeople have strong views on a particular issue, there's no reason why they shouldn't use the platform they have to promote their point, in the same way that we use our position to help in charity work. But as a rule I don't believe that sport should become political. For me, the Olympics is about people coming together. It's about all the good things in life: about working hard, trying to achieve a goal – all the things people should aspire to, and which make a better world.

It may sound like I'm skirting around what some people consider important issues, but I'm just an athlete. I was just there to go racing.

Chapter 17

London Calling . . . But First the America's Cup Beckons Again

The great excitement amongst the GB sailing team that it had performed so well at the Games was enhanced by the anticipation at the prospect of 2012.

The clock began officially to tick down when the mayor of London, Boris Johnson, was handed the Olympic flag by IOC president Jacques Rogge at the ceremony in Beijing, followed by an eight-minute handover presentation. It featured a red double-decker bus, footballer David Beckham and musicians Jimmy Page and Leona Lewis.

An Olympic closing ceremony can leave you feeling anti-climactic, but here it was special as we could now begin to look ahead to London – or, in the case of sailing, Weymouth.

People ask me how long I can continue in dinghy racing. In the Finn, it's difficult to forecast, because it is hard work physically. I'll be 35 by the time of the London Games, and that's probably the limit for that class. I don't think I could go beyond that age in the Finn. Other options would be to go for the Star, the two-handed keelboat. For the helmsman, that is slightly less physically demanding.

But if you try to move to another boat, it can take time to learn the nuances of the new discipline. I was fortunate in that I adapted quickly when I moved to the Finn. But it could require two years to learn aspects of a new class. On balance, the realistic prospect is to stick with the Finn, in which I have all that experience, and try to maintain my fitness.

Why continue in Olympic sailing anyway, considering all the alternatives open to me? The answer is that I will continue to do so while I possess sufficient belief that I can succeed. There is also an important psychological factor in that, once you win gold, you always know you are capable of doing so again.

However, that said, nothing I've done in the past will count for anything at Weymouth in 2012. I don't look back. I endeavour to focus on the here and now and treat every Games, and every Olympic cycle, as my first. You have to clock on afresh every time and leave your last Games far behind. Assuming that all goes to plan, and I go for 2012, it won't be a question of glory-hunting, the pursuit of a fourth gold, even though I'm reminded constantly by friends, relatives and the media of records I could break. And principally that one more gold would put me on a par with Paul Elvström.

The Dane is the most successful Olympic sailor in the sport and the person whose name is most often mentioned when the best sailors in the world are asked to name their inspirational figure. He is a person who is held in the highest regard as a sportsman; a man of integrity and a man of great skill.

He won his first Olympic gold medal in 1948 in the days when the Firefly was the Olympic single-handed class. When the Finn was introduced, he claimed gold in 1952, 1956 and 1960. That record of four golds has yet to be equalled. Remarkably, he went on to compete in a further four Olympics, just missing out on a Star medal at Acapulco in 1968 and a Tornado medal at Los Angeles in 1984 when sailing with his youngest daughter. He is the only sailor in the world to win the world championship in five different classes. Elvström was influential off the water too, producing a series of books on the racing rules and designing components, including the Elvström Life Jacket.

Being able to pass Rodney Pattison's haul of two golds and one silver meant a lot and it was very sporting of Rodney to send me a message very soon after I had won in Beijing.

Of course, the challenges were certainly different in his day. Those competitors weren't professional then; and they had none of the backup we have now. But they had the Corinthian spirit. They'd go out one day, come back in, totally rebuild their boats, sleep overnight in tents, and go out again. It was amazing the developments they made in those years. Rodney was in the forefront of that.

I doubt if Rodney received the welcome fanfare we did, either. Once we got back from Beijing, there were formal receptions to attend. There was a do at Mansion House at which Prime Minister Gordon Brown and his wife Sarah were present. I have met Brown a couple of times and always feel slightly sorry for him as he is much warmer in person than he appears on the television.

It makes sense for the government to try and gain politically from the Olympics' success but it can also lead to some embarrassing moments. Whenever I meet Tessa Jowell for some reason she usually calls me 'Matthew'. On top of that, you get half an hour of political spiel, but if you try and discuss the issues surrounding your sport, you get the feeling she's just not listening. That's when you get annoyed with politicians. Fortunately, British sport has a far better-known figurehead in Lord Coe. I have a lot of respect for him as an athlete, though I'm too young to remember the great races between him and Steve Ovett. He's a great ambassador for sport in the UK.

I quite enjoy reading about politics and watching it all played out. After Beijing, I also got invited to meet Opposition leader David Cameron in his office at Portcullis House, and was very impressed by him. He's out of the Blair mould: a slick, people-person, compared with Gordon Brown, who's clearly not.

Post-Beijing, we received, by far, the biggest reaction to the success of the team that I've known. In part that's because of 2012. For me, that meant more offers to go on TV shows, endorse products, give talks, and make personal appearances. But though it may go against what has seemingly become a national obsession, I've never had any great desire to be on the TV. The exception is the BBC's *Question of Sport*, because I've got a huge interest in all sports. I was on Phil Tufnell's team with Paul Sackey, the England and Wasps rugby player. On Matt Dawson's team were Jimmy Bullard and Rebecca Adlington.

One TV appearance that I wasn't happy about was when I was asked to take part in some filming for an item to be screened as part of the BBC's *Sports Personality of the Year* show later in the year. I had been requested to co-operate in a stunt in which I had to don a dinner suit. That was fine – until I was also asked to fall backwards into Weymouth Harbour. It was autumn, and it was freezing. It was for a sequence in which Rebecca Adlington was also featured, swimming in an evening dress. Except she did that in a swimming pool, which wasn't quite the same.

The piece which was shown was like an out-take and, frankly, came across as more of a piss-take. I was furious with the BBC and it annoys me that some people show such little respect for sailing. They seem to view it as a joke sport because they don't understand it. It's due to ignorance of the highest level.

I avoid the celebrity circuit like the proverbial plague. That fact was reinforced after the Games when I managed to make it on to the gossip pages of the *News of the World*, complete with a rather embarrassing photograph. I was snapped in a nightclub, with a certain young woman, and was well and truly stitched up. It was blown out of all proportion. It gave all my mates something to laugh about, but it was annoying as it caused me plenty of grief for something that was a nothing story.

You want interest for the right reasons. You want to be perceived as someone with good values. Not becoming famous by hanging out with the 'right' people.

Becoming a relatively well-known sportsman shouldn't mean intrusion into my private life. It simply doesn't fit easily with my character. I'm a sportsman, not a celebrity. I couldn't care less if I'm famous or not. I've never gone out and sought fame. That's not why I got into the sport; it's not why I compete. Fortunately, we don't have to deal with some of the issues that footballers do.

Of course, I'm all for sailing receiving good publicity, and increasing its appeal. I think it's important that it is understood better. So, what I do find rather frustrating, as a sailor, is that all the interest tends to centre on more high-profile sports. It's not just my view. I know that a lot of other sailors get really irritated with that, because they don't feel that they get any recognition. It was just a bit galling, after Beijing, that it was all about cycling.

I must stress, I know some of them very well and have great admiration for men like Chris Hoy – now Sir Chris.

I first met Chris on the flight back from the Athens Olympics. We had a good chat about our respective sports and discovered that both our families had made great sacrifices to help us fulfil our careers. I was impressed with his humility about everything he had done. We also shared experiences on the journey back from Beijing.

However, I think it's worth remembering that, at the Beijing Olympics, sailing won more medals that were on the table than cycling did, though at the BBC's *Sports Personality of the Year* show, the cyclists won Team of the Year. I'm not knocking what the cyclists achieved in any way. I just think that sometimes sailing's forgotten a little bit; doesn't have the credibility it should do.

Fortunately, sailing is bigger than the Olympics and world and European championships. We can look forward to the America's Cup and all sorts of other challenges between Olympics. Unlike some Olympians, I will continue after 2012 and still have many other goals afterwards. Frankly, I'm far more interested in furthering my sailing career outside of the Olympic arena, with the America's Cup being the primary goal. What I won't be doing is sitting around brooding, saying 'Why am I not getting as much attention as him?' or 'Why am I not on this or that TV show?' I gave up on that a long time ago.

I really don't like the idea of talking myself up, anyway. It doesn't sit easily with me to have interviewers talking about records and asking 'What makes you the best?' As a sportsman, I find nothing more irritating than other sportspeople shouting about how good they are, or how great they could be. I guess some do it psychologically to give themselves more confidence.

I respect the people who work hard and get the results they deserve, and prove themselves. It's not about what you *could* do. On the whole, the leader board, like the league table, doesn't lie.

One of the most satisfying aspects after Beijing was people stopping you in the street, and wanting to congratulate you. That's never happened to me before. As a sailor, that's quite a leap forward. I even had a London cabbie not only insisting on shaking my hand, but refusing to accept the fare!

But 'fame' can have its downside as well as advantages. In the past I've protected my privacy zealously. It's a fine balance. I've opened up more as I get older, in terms of interviews, and realised what's expected of somebody in my position.

Media coverage has changed significantly even since I started out. There are the dedicated sailing journalists, but they are becoming fewer and fewer. They've always been sympathetic to the cause. They tended to be pretty supportive because it's in their own interest to push the sport and generally looked after you. When non-sailing journalists began to take an interest, you weren't really sure if you could trust them, or whether their real motive was just to have a dig at sailing. Back then, when people didn't know so much about sailing, and even now, to an extent, there's still an elitist tag hanging over the sport, and I felt very much that I had to be wary about being stitched up.

Throughout my career, though, I have to say I've been very fortunate. There are very few times I have read something and felt like I've been turned over (and one of those times was with a sailing journalist, anyway). I believe that's because I've tried to maintain a sense of equanimity about what I've done. I feel you've got to keep yourself balanced between the ups and the downs. It's fine being brash and talking the talk when you're doing well, and go out and win a gold medal. I'm sure journalists love that. But as soon as that guy has a tough period then it gets turned around pretty quickly.

But I understand that the more high profile you get, the more you're going to have to take that kind of thing, because it's going to happen. You just ignore it. Or possibly use it to motivate yourself – just as I did when there was a lot of talk before the pre-Beijing trials. What Ed Wright was quoted as saying in the press did actually fire me up quite a bit. There was that underlying tone there of 'Ah, yes, but was Ben going to be any good when he comes back from the America's Cup?' Instead of getting riled, I used it to my advantage.

These days, exposure is important in terms of your sponsors. Over the years I have been extremely fortunate to have been supported by some great businesses and brands, such as current sponsors JP Morgan Asset Management, BT, Henri Lloyd, Volvo and Corum Watches. Whilst the financial support is crucial it is also a real confidence boost to know that you have so many people backing you and supporting you. I have also been lucky enough to build some strong relationships with successful businessmen like Paul Strzelecki whose family own the Henri Lloyd clothing business and Campbell Fleming, the CEO of JP Morgan Asset Management in the UK. It's nice to be able to call on people like that for advice.

After Beijing, the interest in us from many quarters was crazy for a month; then suddenly it all dissipated, albeit reappearing briefly around the time of the *Sports Personality of the Year* just before Christmas.

In the aftermath of Atlanta, when there had been similar excitement for a while, there had been what I'd describe as a 'Now what?' vacuum. There had been nothing to do; there were no events. I even had a break from training. If you allow it, there can be a big void in your life. That was why, after Sydney and Athens, it suited me to go straight down to New Zealand to train with America's Cup teams. Yes, I missed all the post-Olympics euphoria and appearances on TV shows. But, in a way, that didn't worry me. I much prefer to get away from all the razzamatazz, and keep sailing; try and get back to some normality, rather than dwell on the events of the summer.

I was soon back on the water again, as I joined Sir Richard Branson on his latest record-breaking attempt, about which I will reveal more later. There was also a new America's Cup project to keep me occupied.

One thing is for sure about my life: the travelling rarely stops. I'm fortunate that I have never really struggled with homesickness. On the contrary, from the moment I set off on this career path there was a real excitement about going to new countries and events. It's many years now from that day when, as a teenager, I flew out to Tokyo for those youth world championships, and I still love travelling today. Mind you, Japan was very different back then. There were no signs in English anywhere. Trying to navigate on the rail system was completely impossible. As far as I could establish, when they say 'yes' they mean 'no'! I didn't work that out for a week! It was such a weird experience at such a young age.

The first time I went to New Zealand was in 1993. I was only 15, and really excited about it because it was such a long way from home and I'd heard so much about Auckland in particular, and its enormous harbour, known as the City of Sails. I was amazed at how green that country is.

Not all places you compete in are glamorous. Far from it. The Laser world championships in 1997 were in Chile, at a place called Algarrobo, two and a half hours west of Santiago, on the coast. It was incredibly backward. The back of beyond. It was supposed to be one of the area's top resorts but it was pretty rough. We stayed in a really old hotel, but the place appeared to be falling down. One night we had an earthquake; just a tremor, really. Everyone was worried there was going to be a tsunami, so, in the middle of the night, in pouring rain, they started running for safety up the hill. I just stayed in my room. I was quite high up anyway, and thought I'd be OK.

It was the first time I'd been to somewhere that you describe as Third World. Coming from a wealthy nation, it opened my eyes to how some of the world exists. There was absolutely nothing in this town, so we drove to another one where there was supposed to be a supermarket, to try and get some muesli bars, things like that. We drove down this coast road, stopped, and came across a little old woman. It was torrential rain, and she was standing there in a big smock, water dripping off her. She held her hand out. I'd no idea how long she'd been there. I had some bread in my hand. That's all I had. I offered it to her, and she snatched it from me. She was so happy to have some food. It was the first time I'd really experienced extreme poverty.

In places like that, all the sailors tend to end up staying at the same place. There's no other option. Some foreign sailors you get on with. Some you don't. In general, there's a sense of camaraderie in sailing, especially in single-handed classes. You're all doing the same thing, travelling around on your own. Unless you're a real loner, it's good to chat.

The first time I went to the Middle East was to Kuwait, in 1996, after Atlanta. Its tourist board invited all the top Laser sailors there, and there was a $10,000 first prize. That was a huge amount of money to a 19-year-old then. But there was nothing there. God knows why Saddam Hussein wanted to invade the place. Oh, yes. Oil, I suppose. It was the first time I'd experienced a culture without alcohol, and no women. By that, I meant they weren't allowed to look at you, or you at them. Even in a burger bar, there'd be a special lane for women to order their food so they'd have no contact with you. I found it very strange.

After three days, it was so boring, you just wanted to get out of this place. It helped a little that I managed to win. But then the organisers said: 'If you want your money, we've got it in cash, but you'll get it after we've held this Optimist event for youngsters. You'll need to wait another three days until that's over.' So, we had to hang around. I was sharing a room with Hamish Pepper, the brilliant New Zealand sailor. Spending three days trying to find something to do in Kuwait wasn't fun.

Some of this may sound like something out of a TV travelogue. But you're there to do a job and race, and train and prepare to race. My approach is simple: you're not there on holiday. You're not there to go sightseeing. In China, for example, I didn't visit anywhere during the Beijing Games. Not even the Great Wall.

Some places we sailors visit a lot because so many events are held there, such as San Francisco, Sydney, Auckland, you get to know them quite well. So, you know the best places to hang out, and where to stay. The hardest part is the difficulty of staying in touch with families, and maintaining relationships. I've been pretty much living out of a suitcase for thirteen years. That's quite difficult at times. You miss having a normal home life, with a normal routine.

It's just a completely different existence from most people; indeed, even most sportsmen. I suppose a golfer's schedule comes closest to mine. It's really quite crazy. It sounds blasé, but you get to know the airports around the world and where the best coffee shops are. Flying is always a bit of a struggle, but at least I am based in Europe. Many of my Kiwi mates frequently fly from New Zealand up to Europe and back for a five-day regatta. They are seriously racking up the air miles.

But to return to the America's Cup. Whether I will get the opportunity to compete in one with a British-based team – and, more crucially, when – has, at the time of writing, still not been fully resolved. There has been protracted legal wrangling over the staging of the thirty-third America's Cup, between the American syndicate BMW Oracle Racing, owned by the American computer magnate Larry Ellison, and the cup holder Alinghi.

All I know is that when we do get the go-ahead we can look forward to it with optimism.

The delay has been particularly frustrating as the TeamOrigin project had been progressing so well. As I intimated earlier, though I'd had experience with two America's Cup teams, one had been American and the other New Zealand-based, and I was still determined to be part of a British challenge. It was a desire I shared with Iain Percy. Ever since we competed in our first Games together back in Sydney, it had always been a common goal to do the America's Cup as a partnership in a British team.

It almost happened after the 2000 Games, with Peter Harrison's GB challenge. In the event, I was too young and Ian Walker became the skipper. As I have described, I joined up with the OneWorld team, albeit briefly; then, after Athens, played a part in the New Zealand project.

It was in 2005 that I first met Sir Keith Mills at a Confederation of British Industry (CBI) conference at the Royal

Albert Hall. Keith had his 2012 hat on, and I was asked to do a Q&A session with him. Sir Keith had been appointed international president and CEO of London 2012, the company that was established to bid for the 2012 Olympic Games. Together with Lord Coe, he was responsible for developing what had turned out to be a successful bid strategy when London saw off competition from New York, Paris, Madrid and Moscow.

A successful businessman who founded Air Miles in 1988, Sir Keith has a great reputation in the world of sport and is also a very keen amateur sailor. In 1999, he was one of the crew that won the Clipper Round the World race. He is also the principal investor in Alex Thomson Racing, the management company for the British solo sailor, Alex Thomson, and the Hugo Boss Open 60 team. The same year that we first met, 2005, Sir Keith received a number of awards including Master Entrepreneur of the Year, Chief Executive of the Year and the Sports Industry Businessman of the Year.

During that CBI conference, Sir Keith asked me questions about the London bid, and what bringing the Olympics to London would mean to me and the sailing fraternity. The session went well, and we got on really well. We had a quick chat afterwards, and he mentioned that he was very keen on doing the America's Cup one day. We parted with him saying: 'I'll give you a call if it looks like I can make anything happen.' It was as vague as that, but I was delighted. He was the man to take that on, if anybody. But we left it at that. Obviously he had a lot on with the 2012 bid.

I felt he was a man I could work with. He's such a gentleman, very polite and well mannered, but with a steely, determined glint in his eye. The success he's had gives everyone else confidence.

We kept in touch. In the meantime, Keith got involved with the RYA and with its chairman Rod Carr and started doing feasibility studies, and identifying designers.

The following year, 2006, Iain Percy and I had a meeting with Keith to discuss what potentially we could do. He was keen to elicit our views on what was needed to win an America's Cup – although, of course, they were very informal and discreet discussions because we were both heavily involved with America's Cup teams for 2007. I was with Team New Zealand, while Iain was helmsman of the Italian +39 team in which, incidentally, Bart Simpson was a member of his afterguard.

Keith had started the ball rolling, and now had additional backing from TeamOrigin partner and investor, Charles Dunstone – the man who founded the Carphone Warehouse – who by now had thrown his hat into the ring. During that 2007 America's Cup, Keith was a prominent figure down in Valencia, talking to potential sponsors. In that period he recruited Mike Sanderson as team director.

A New Zealander, Mike is a phenomenally experienced sailor. He had been mainsheet trimmer in the 1995, 2000 and 2003 America's Cups, with Tag Heuer (skippered by Chris Dickson), Team New Zealand (Dean Barker) and BMW Oracle Racing (Peter Holmberg) respectively. Having won the 1993–4 Whitbread Round the World race as trimmer aboard *New Zealand Endeavour*, skippered by Grant Dalton, he won the 2005–6 Volvo Ocean Race as skipper aboard *ABN AMRO 1*. It led to him winning the 2006 ISAF World Sailor of the Year award.

After the 2007 America's Cup was over, Keith and I came to an agreement that I would be the skipper and helmsman of

TeamOrigin. Our campaign to win the America's Cup could begin in earnest.

I had no reservations about the project, despite what happened to the last GB challenge. As I've said, that was slightly late and underfunded. I never felt those guys were given enough of a chance to do it properly. But now there were people like myself, and Bart and Iain; talented British sailors who'd been gaining experience in the America's Cup with different teams. It was obvious that we could put a strong sailing team together. With Keith's and Mike's expertise, and an extremely talented designer, an Argentinian named Juan Kouyoumdjian (not surprisingly better known as 'Juan K'), it was a very strong unit – one potentially capable of winning the Cup.

Chapter 18

America's Cup Potential Confirmed

There will probably be some people, particularly in these cash-strapped times for many, who will consider the America's Cup to be an indulgent irrelevance; that it is a trophy squabbled over by a few extremely wealthy, ego-driven characters.

Yes, it tends attracts some of the world's most flamboyant yachtsmen-entrepreneurs, but in fact, the America's Cup is one of the most desirable sporting trophies in the world and the pinnacle of yacht racing. Perhaps I'm a little obsessive about it; but then I'm a patriotic Briton, with a feel for my country's maritime history. Certainly, whenever I walk through, or drive through, Trafalgar Square, I always have a good look at Nelson's Column. It's like an act of homage. He's a real hero figure to me.

There's something about the nostalgia of the America's Cup that appeals to me; this event which started around the Isle of Wight, with that challenge by the Earl of Wilton, the commodore of Britain's Royal Yacht Squadron, to the commodore of the New York Yacht Club in 1851 to race as part of an Industrial World Fair, otherwise known as Prince Albert's Great Exhibition. It is said that when Queen Victoria asked who was second, after the yacht *America* passed the finishing line eight minutes ahead of the British fleet, the solemn reply came: 'There is no second, ma'am.'

Our nation's determination to win back the trophy saw the development of the America's Cup. Yet, over 150 years on, Britain still hasn't won it, and that rankles. We should have done so by now, but we've never been close. There's no reason why we can't assemble a team that's successful, or at least with a chance of winning, because there's some highly talented sailors here. I have no doubt that when that eventually happens people in Britain will develop more interest in the racing. To win would be a source of huge national pride. Switzerland may be a landlocked nation, but when they won the Cup it was still greeted by great celebration.

With a few notable exceptions, there aren't that many of my Olympic peers who have competed in the America's Cup as well. You can boast all the skills as an Olympic sailor, and possess exceptional raw talent, but it often surprises small-boat sailors what a contrast it is, moving into the big boats. It's that whole team environment and the technical side of big-boat sailing that takes a while to pick up on. It's a hard step to take. And another thing: it's always a gamble when you take time away from your Olympic career to get involved in big-boat sailing. There's always the fear that when you return you'll be off the pace for the next Games. So, regardless of where we're placed with our America's Cup challenge, come the build-up to 2012, there's no way I'd miss a home Olympics.

TeamOrigin started out with the goal to win the Cup even if that took two campaigns and a huge investment.

One of the most fascinating aspects for me is that the sailing team does have a significant impact on design philosophy. We say where the boat has to be strong; whether going downwind or upwind, or at the start. There are always trade-offs. If you make a gain in one area, then inevitably you'll lose it somewhere else. You accept that. It may be, say, that you end up with a boat that doesn't manoeuvre particularly well, but goes ten per cent quicker. You'd always take that. Even if you started last, you could sail round your opponent. But these things have to be agreed upon. It is not just left to the design team.

Once the boat is built, the real trick is tuning it to a fine pitch. Again similar to a Formula 1 car, the focus is on getting one hundred per cent out of the product of the design to generate maximum speed. I can't design a boat, but I do have a fair amount of input on getting it to perform at its optimum. Where we, the crew, are important is providing feedback on the feel of the boat once it is in the water. It can be that the first time you sail it, the balance is completely wrong. In which case, we chop it up – not literally – and make some pretty drastic changes. One option, say, would be to move the mast forwards or backwards. Or move the keel. Though hopefully not, bearing in mind the logistics of shifting twenty tons, but it does happen.

For the last Cup, when I was with Team New Zealand, we had great designers, and fortunately both our boats were really well balanced. All our biggest gains were the result of sail depth and through the fins on the keel (the keel bulb gives boat stability, and the lift comes from the keel fins which stop the boat slipping sideways. The thicker it is the more lift you get, but the more induced drag you get.)

Once the British challenge had been named, as TeamOrigin, offices were opened in Valencia and Portsmouth. Then Mike and Iain and I started to get the sailing team together. I should stress that I was really careful not to just get a bunch of mates around, with the aim of all having a great time. What is important is to identify sailors who you can trust and respect. That is something we all have for each other.

The most important aspect was getting the afterguard right. Apart from Iain Percy, Bart Simpson and myself, the crew included Ian Moore, the navigator, who had sailed with me for Team New Zealand; mastman George Skuodas, a very experienced Olympic and America's Cup sailor; Matt Cornwell, who was our bowman; and Neil MacDonald, well known for his Whitbread and Volvo Ocean Race exploits. There was Rob Greenhalgh who's a very talented small-boat sailor. He sails 18ft skiffs really fast, and has been world champion in those. He sailed with Mike Sanderson in the last Volvo Ocean Race which they won and has a lot of experience at a relatively young age. And there are other characters like Chris Brittle, one of the grinders, an ex-Finn sailor, and a real physical specimen.

We aimed to get the top guys in the world. Simple as that. Some were Olympic sailors, some had a background in big boats, and match-racing, performance dinghies, but not necessarily Olympic backgrounds.

If you target the best, you tend to ensure mutual respect throughout the crew. While we wanted to keep the British identity as strong as possible, we also got in some really good Kiwis who had won an America's Cup before or Round the World races; absolutely the top guys in the game in their positions. It was a good blend of older experience and young talent. And loads of enthusiasm.

There was also an Aussie, an Irishman, a Dane and a Frenchman (believe it or not, given my experiences with one of his compatriots!), but nobody that I'd describe as totally alien. Predominantly it was a British team, but I think it's good to have different nationalities; guys with a slightly different approach, like New Zealanders.

In Britain, it's fair to say there's a (begrudging) admiration for Kiwis. Probably that's partly because of the fearsome reputation of the All Blacks. But it's also the same in the sailing fraternity. Every New Zealander we had has won an America's Cup, so there was enormous esteem for them within the team.

The helmsman's relationship with the design team is ultra-important, just as the driver's is in Formula 1. Also like motorsport there are certain parameters you have to work within.

But within the limitations, the designer, utilising the benefits of computer modelling, then attempts to develop the best hull shape. There's also a rig designer who does exactly the same. From that, the sail designer gets to work. Everything has to match. The way the rules work, if you have a boat that's slightly different, then the mast has to be slightly different, and the sails then have to be slightly different. It requires good communication by the design team.

Our chief designer, Juan K, was responsible for the top boat in the last two ocean races, and worked with BMW in the last Cup.

Our first step in preparing for the next America's Cup was when a crew representing TeamOrigin took part in the King Edward VII Gold Cup, a regatta in Bermuda, part of the World Match-Racing Tour. That series of regattas is similar to America's Cup racing, except in smaller boats, with crews of three to six. We finished third, and were delighted with that. It was a good exercise because we'd been out of match-racing for eighteen months, due to my Olympic preparations, and we'd never sailed together as a team. The crew was Iain Percy, Matt Cornwell (bowman), and a trimmer from Denmark called Christian Kamp.

It takes a while to re-familiarise yourself with the manoeuvring and the rules. I'm relatively new to match-racing, but gradually I'm finding it easier to switch comfortably between different size yachts, and understanding the nuances of that boat. You also rely a lot on trimmers to have a good feel of the boat as well and set it up to its optimum efficiency.

We also entered two America's Cup version 5 regattas. The first was at the Club Náutico Español de Vela annual regatta at Valencia in November, when we competed in America's Cup boats. Considering we were in a borrowed boat and we'd never sailed together as a team before, we did really well. Alinghi, the America's Cup defenders, won comfortably. We won the first race, and finished third overall, just behind the Italian team Luna Rossa. We beat the Spanish challenger, whose boat we were borrowing. But as Mike Sanderson said afterwards: 'Our aim is to win the America's Cup, and that is not done in an instant.'

Even then I felt we had the team to do the job – whenever that was. That faith was vindicated to a great extent down in New Zealand when we took part in the Louis Vuitton Pacific Series at Auckland. This was as close as you can get to America's Cup sailing, and with so many of us having done this type of event before it brought a huge amount of confidence to the team. With that experience aboard the boat, people believed we were going in the right direction.

The Louis Vuitton Pacific Series, a new event, was contested by both former and potential America's Cup teams, in January and February 2009. The final entry list for the regatta consisted of ten teams representing nine countries. As well as Alinghi, there were familiar names including the hosts, Emirates Team New Zealand, BMW Oracle Racing and Luna Rossa. It was match-racing, one on one, using two Team New Zealand and two BMW Oracle boats from the last America's Cup.

It was still a daunting proposition for us, though. As a team, we weren't able to get together to do any training beforehand. All the other teams were preparing down in Valencia before going to New Zealand. However, we were allotted two hours a day for five days before the event, and in that time we got a huge amount of work in.

The focus that everyone had was really pleasing. We got to the first race, raring to go. We started off in great style, winning every race in Pool B in the first round. That included beating Alinghi, and Luna Rossa. We went through to the next round and again were beating Alinghi, but unfortunately down the final run we had one bad gybe which allowed them to get past. Our next race was against BMW Oracle, skippered by Russell Coutts. We had a good start and they had a penalty, but unfortunately the forestay broke and we couldn't hoist the headsail.

We beat Luna Rossa again, in the most exciting match of the series so far, winning by just four seconds, and then were seven seconds too good for Emirates Team New Zealand. It was great to take on Dean Barker and the guys. Then we lost to the Italian team, Damiani Italia, after it was adjudged that we were over the line. It meant we had to turn back and restart which gave the Italian boat an advantage from which we never recovered.

We reached the quarter-finals, but lost narrowly to Damiani Italia. By the end, we were a little disappointed we didn't get further than we did, considering the teams that we had beaten.

To take on all the top teams showed a lot of potential. Hopefully it's what we can expect when multi-challenger America's Cup racing once again goes ahead.

One of the most encouraging things I took out of the regatta down in Auckland was the team cohesion. In a way, it was a big relief that everyone got on so well. We had wanted to pick a team that had experience, youthfulness, talent, but also personalities that gel, and it did.

Of course, I felt a certain pride about being skipper of a British America's Cup team. That had so long been my goal. But in the long term that will not be enough. I am determined that a GB boat will claim the prize that has always eluded this country. 'Defeated skipper' is something I'd prefer not to have on my CV.

For me, that means doing a good job, not just on but off the water, of galvanising the whole team of diverse talents to perform.

The skipper of these yachts can actually be anyone on the boat. It's the equivalent of the captain of a ball sport. It's not a question of standing there and yelling, but keeping everyone going; maintaining the right tempo and ensuring everyone works towards a common goal. However, *normally* it makes sense for the skipper to be the helmsman because he has the final decision on where the boat goes; he calls the mark-rounding manoeuvres, in conjunction with the tactician.

The period of time with Team New Zealand on the B boat was in a way critical for me. I grew up a lot in that position. It was difficult; there were guys who weren't happy because they weren't in the A team. There were days when we were basically getting whipped, when we just had to go out to wash the laundry. It was tough, but we made it work. We did a really good job, I believe, as a group of people on that boat. I learnt a huge amount from that, and working with Grant Dalton and Dean Barker, even though there were some things I thought could have been done better. But that in itself was an important part of my education.

I did give my style of leadership quite a lot of thought. We Brits – and that goes for the Kiwis, too – don't generally go in for the big high-fives, and the ra-ra-ra style. We're more restrained. For me, it's more about leading by example. And for that, I looked at Russell Coutts who has set the standard in the last fifteen years. He has been an incredibly successful sailor, so he has the respect of the other guys. It's a bit like that old football expression: 'Show us yer medals.' Players tend to respect a manager who's achieved success at the highest level on the field himself. It's like that with Russell. In return, he treats everyone with respect, but is also very firm about why the team's there. And that's to win, and not take the easy options.

It's about keeping everyone focussed over a long period. It's about communication. Making clear what we want to achieve every time we go out. The people on the boat have all been successful in their own right. You're not dealing with novices. So, it's more about empowering them, and letting them get on with it.

Outside sailing, I love watching other sports, and sporting leaders, and reading about them. I learn from what the best do well, but also from what some *don't* do well. You can admire Martin Johnson, as England rugby captain. On the other hand, I look at Sir Nick Faldo, Europe captain at the last Ryder Cup. A great player in his day, but when it came to leading a team, it all seemed far too much about him rather than the guys who were out there, trying to retain the Cup. You kept saying to yourself: 'What is he doing?'

With that in mind, it's a fair question to ask: does being a great sailor necessarily mean you will become a great skipper and leader of men?

I understand that there's no way I'm going to win it on my own. Iain's got to make the right call about where to go on the course, and the pitman has got to make sure that the spinnaker goes up properly. Everyone's got to work together.

It's like Formula 1 when you hear drivers refer constantly to 'we'. That's not just politeness to the engineers and mechanics. It's correct. I'm very conscious that it's 'we' as a team. Not about 'I'. The only time I have referred to 'I' was when it was a cock-up that I made!

In that Louis Vuitton race against Damiani Italia, when we were over the line at the start, that was down to one man. You have to put your hand up. I admitted that it was my fault, or words to that effect!

Being skipper also means harnessing the team's potential by saying the right things in the meetings beforehand, using the right tone, setting the right goals. Iain was part of that process too.

When we arrived in New Zealand, I accepted that, considering what little practice we had and the fact that we were a new team, it was unlikely that we were going to beat these rivals. Nevertheless we had quite clear goals on how well we thought we could do, and what we should work on and improve. We actually left New Zealand with a very positive attitude.

When we will be able to capitalise on that progress we had made was always going to be ultimately dependent on the litigation between Alinghi and BMW Oracle being resolved satisfactorily. And for them to stop firing broadsides at each other.

Now that the courts have ruled that the next America's Cup will be a head to head between the holders Alinghi and Oracle, as 'the challengers of record', the other teams just hope they can organise that contest quickly so the rest of us can join in for the thirty-fourth Cup.

Hopefully, they will race in February 2010, possibly in Valencia, although Alinghi would like it to be later. The legal battle has been damaging for the competition and many of the teams and Sir Keith has done an incredible job in the circumstances to hold TeamOrigin together. Throughout, he worked hard with the two teams involved, in the hope that they could work their way through this problem.

It all meant, though, that Sir Keith was forced to scale down TeamOrigin activities. As a sailor and competitor the current situation is about as frustrating as it gets. It's hard to watch the reputation of the sport being so badly damaged, but it is not the first time this has happened in the long history of the Cup. I doubt it will be the last.

Chapter 19

On Wind and a Prayer: A Record-Breaking Attempt

Preparing for the next America's Cup was necessarily slow progress. The same couldn't be said of the moment when, a couple of months after Beijing, I suddenly found myself involved in a transatlantic record attempt. I was quoted beforehand as saying that I expected 'a pretty wild ride'. I would not be disappointed. It turned out to be an awesome experience, one I won't forget in a hurry. Richard Branson's boat, *Virgin Money*, was definitely built for speed, not for comfort.

It all came about through my connection with Mike Sanderson. He was associated with a US owner, Alex Jackson, a wealthy hedge-fund manager from New York, who wanted to build the biggest, fastest monohull possible. Juan K, who, as I've mentioned before, is our TeamOrigin America's Cup designer, was commissioned to design *Speedboat*, as she was called, and Mike project-managed it. The yacht lived up to its name.

Built entirely of carbon fibre, including the sails, in order to keep the weight to a minimum, the 100ft supermaxi, costing more than £7 million, was twice as powerful as any other boat around, capable of speeds in excess of 45 knots.

The boat was built in Auckland, where Alex Jackson did a bit of sailing with her, but not that much. His sole aim was to sail fast and break records, and, with that in mind, he went to Virgin boss Richard Branson with the prospect of doing a transatlantic record attempt.

That was really all you could do with her. She was too big to race round the 'cans', and was really designed for long-distance races like the Sydney-Hobart, or Fastnet. Or record attempts like this.

Richard had done the transatlantic powerboat Blue Riband back in 1986, a record which still stands, and had piloted hot-air balloons across the Atlantic and Pacific. But he hadn't attempted another record-breaking attempt for several years, so this really appealed to him. So, *Speedboat* became *Virgin Money*.

Mike was skipper, and he asked me to go along as one of the watch captains. I told him I was very keen – as long as I could fit it in with my schedule of post-Olympic commitments. It was to be crewed by several of the TeamOrigin sailing team, together with Alex Jackson, and three of his friends, all amateurs, and Richard and his two grown-up children, Sam and Holly. In all, there would be sixteen talented professionals on board, and eight 'amateurs'.

Of course, you can't all just turn up, and hope for the best. It would be a question of waiting for the right weather window. The boat had been in New York Harbour for three or four months when the call came. We had all been getting on with our lives. I was actually attending a sponsors meeting in Geneva when I got the phone call that the wind was right and the boat would be leaving the following morning.

I caught the last flight from Switzerland out to New York, and arrived at 1 a.m. I hadn't eaten, and was still dressed in smart trousers, jacket and shoes. I got in a taxi and went straight to the marina which is downtown, close to where the World Trade Center stood. Initially, the cabbie couldn't find it. Eventually we arrived, I jumped aboard and, at around 4 a.m. we departed – ahead of schedule to try and catch the back end of a weather system as we left New York.

Fortunately, I found some spare sailing kit to use. It was bizarre. I'd never even been on the boat. We had a safety briefing in the Hudson before we got the sails up and headed for the start line at the Ambrose lighthouse, just off Long Island.

It's a strange experience, sailing down the Hudson at night, and looking back at the city. It was cold, and there was a strong wind. We would need plenty of the latter. We just had the mainsail up, and were running down out of the river, and, to give an idea of the potential performance of her, we flew past a cargo ship, a car transporter which was going at full speed out of the harbour, probably at around 20 knots.

And then we were off, straight into the record attempt. We needed to complete the journey of 2,925 nautical miles to Lizard Point in less than 6 days, 17 hours, 52 minutes and 39 seconds – the time set, ironically enough, by Mike Sanderson in 2003, aboard the yacht *Mari-Cha IV*. There was a good weather forecast, and we were ripping along that first night. Unbelievable stuff. We had 25–30 knots of wind behind us, and the boat just took off, absolutely flat out.

The weather is absolutely crucial. The navigator Stan Honey had a huge task but is one of the most respected sailors around. At that time of year, the second half of October, you're basically trying to piggyback on a low-pressure band going across the

Atlantic, and ride it all the way across. It's rather like a surfer catching the right wave.

It's vital that you stay on that track because if you fall off a weather pattern, then all bets are off. You don't know what's going to come next.

We had to fight really hard to keep to the course required to break the record. The wind was powerful enough, but not quite in the right direction, which meant that the boat was out of balance and steering the thing was extraordinarily tough work.

It was gruelling, even though we were only at the helm at certain times. We had watch patterns: three hours on, three hours on standby and ready to go if needed, and three hours off, when you could sleep. Physically, I'd never sailed a boat which took that much effort. And, to be quite honest, I simply wasn't really prepared for it.

Stupidly, I didn't have any gloves – the consequence partly of my rushed departure, I should stress, although I wouldn't normally use them for steering big boats – so I wore the skin off my hands. They ended up pretty swollen and with massive blisters. I also got really bad tendonitis in my right wrist, purely because of the load of the boat. I was in a really bad way. I had to go grovelling to Holly Branson, who had qualified as a doctor the year before and was the boat's medic, to try and get some treatment.

It wasn't pleasant, even if you were below deck. And certainly not for those unfamiliar with ocean sailing. There was a really violent motion of the boat because it was travelling so quickly. The noise it generates is just unbelievable. The structure is amazing. It's basically designed to flex. The boat is so big and travelling at such speeds that, if it stayed taut, it wouldn't be able to take the loading. It's a pretty bizarre feeling. You just think there's no way this boat's going to take these forces for five days. It can't handle it. But structurally, it was fine.

Another time, I'd been up at the bow, helping out. We came back and I actually put my hand on the inner forestay to steady myself. Just as I did that, the guy in the cockpit started furling the sail. They have powered winches on these boats. My arm got caught inside the sail, and it was getting tighter and tighter. Fortunately, they heard me shouting. Another couple of seconds and it would have broken my arm. That was a close call, but it shows how easily things can go wrong.

Despite all that, it was a fun boat to sail – if seriously hard work. It's such a powerful boat that it really beats everyone up. It's like trying to tame a monster. Helming it the second night was the most exhilarating sailing I've ever done. It was a bit like being on a fairground ride. You get to the top of a roller coaster and start feeling the wind coming under your chin, and your stomach starts to part company from the remainder of your body, and you feel intense anticipation.

It was a strange experience steering her, what we call 'weather-helming' because the boat always wants to turn to windward. So, you're steering against it to keep the boat going straight. That's fine, normally. Except this wasn't a normal situation. In the middle of the night, you can't see anything and you're going off the wind angle display on the mast in front of you; but you can deal with that until you go through one of these huge waves at 35 knots. The boat starts shuddering and takes off, and you're desperately holding on, but there's spray everywhere for five seconds and you can't even see your instruments.

These boats only have a very narrow wind angle you can sail at before you wipe out, one way or the other. You're just praying that when you come through one of these waves on the other side, you've got the boat at the right angle. I was just in awe of the fact that the boat could do that.

It was windy and rough, with waves up to forty feet, and winds up to 40 knots, but I wouldn't describe those as extreme conditions. The hull itself was certainly capable of dealing with anything thrown at it. The worst that could happen was that you could end up losing the mast. All ocean-racing boats have a keel, so the boat will always come upright. Of course, if the keel came off then you would have problems, but that was unlikely. Catamarans and trimarans are more dangerous because they can flip over pretty easily.

Two and half days into the attempt, we were going fine, and just on coure for the record when we had a problem with the way the mainsail was reefed (you reduce the mainsail area if it's *too* windy, otherwise the boat blows over).

We'd taken down quite a lot because it was so windy, but the problem was the massive amount of spray produced by the boat was going into the excess main which was coiled up along the boom. The spray and wind combined were wearing away the mainsail. As much as we tried to prevent that, we didn't do a good enough job. If I had a criticism it was that the boat hadn't really done enough miles or hours and hadn't been put through its paces enough before the record attempt for this problem to have become apparent.

The mainsail basically just destroyed itself, and the spinnaker was damaged too. Also a large wave striking the boat from behind washed one of the life rafts overboard. And that was it. We tried to repair the mainsail, but the bottom of it was too badly ripped. It was a tough call to abandon the attempt, but there was no alternative, particularly as a high had developed and we were going to have to skirt around that, so I think, in truth, we would have been struggling to beat the record anyway. If the conditions were right, and you could keep the boat in one piece, you could obliterate the record.

We had a quick get-together of the watch captains and Mike, and the boat's owner, Alex Jackson. Though everybody was disappointed that we'd have to pull out, there was also a bit of relief that the constant hammering was over. The only other decision was whether or not to get the boat back to New York, about two and half days away on the wind, which would have been pretty horrible. The alternative was running down to St George, Bermuda, which was about twenty hours downwind, and beautiful sailing conditions.

It was a no-brainer. We were trying to find as many excuses as possible to go to Bermuda when Richard Branson intervened.

'Bermuda? I think that's on the way to Necker Island, isn't it?' That's Richard's private island, in the British Virgin Islands.

So, that was the decision made! We'd head there.

It was great fun, while it lasted. And, hopefully, there'll be another chance to break that record. There were some great people aboard. The Bransons are really good value. You can't help but admire Richard. He did a lot of work with the media, obviously. PR is his forte. And he worked tirelessly on that. He's generally quiet, and can take a detached view of proceedings. But if necessary he's not afraid to make his voice heard. Just as it must be with the various entities of the Virgin brand, he delegates, but knows when to step in.

There was one typical moment of Branson unflappability. We went down below, and got on the satellite phone, as he had scheduled an interview with ITN.

Try to imagine the scene. With the wind blowing at about 35

knots, the boat's all over the place and even down below it's pretty rough and loads of people are throwing up. Richard calls up, and gets some woman on the other end.

'Hello, ITN,' she says.

'Hello, it's Richard Branson here. I was asked to call this number to do an interview.'

'Richard who?'

'It's Sir Richard Branson here. I'm sailing in the middle of the Atlantic Ocean and I'm supposed to call this number.'

'No, sorry. Don't know anything about it.'

I half-expected him to lose his cool.

Eventually, he got through. Then the phone kept cutting out. But he was incredibly patient, very professional. I was very impressed with him. But then I guess he didn't become such a success without understanding how to deal with the media . . .

He's a self-deprecating, down-to-earth sort of guy, who doesn't take himself too seriously, which was nice. A lovely family, too. We eventually ended up in Bermuda, where his wife Joan was waiting.

In retrospect, I didn't realise how demanding the boat would be to steer. I hadn't got my head around how tough it would be. In fact, it was quite a good learning experience for me. You can't just rock up and sail a boat like that. I wasn't even mentally prepared for it; hadn't even thought about it, to be honest.

Chapter 20

What Voyages Lie Ahead?

At the end of 2008 I travelled to Madrid for the ISAF World Sailor of the Year awards. It was a real honour to win the award for a third time, following a great year. I was really pleased that my parents were able to make it over for the evening.

Life has changed so much in nearly twenty years on the water. It's strange. When I was younger, I could remember all the races I did. That was certainly true of my first Olympics, because I had so much more time to sit and contemplate how I was doing. Now, I can hardly remember the race I did last week. It's straight on to the next event. It's rather sad in a way.

That's why I have enjoyed telling my story. You recall experiences that were fantastic, a few disappointing, occasionally embarrassing! It's nice to look back on what's been achieved but also to look to the future and what challenges lie ahead.

Would I have changed anything? I will preface the following by saying that I don't have any regrets. But if I had to be hyper-self-critical, certainly I was too much in a hurry at times in my sailing. I was too impatient to get on, and definitely when it came to the America's Cup. In hindsight, the first one was completely the wrong thing for me. I probably should have started with a British team in which I had people supporting me and backing me up. Instead I walked into it, unprepared. I had no idea what I was letting myself in for.

The only consolation is that it set me up and prepared me for future involvement in Cup teams.

That decision then was based on advice I took. I've always believed you should seek guidance from people you respect. My view has not changed on that, even though sometimes it turns out to be not right for you at the time. One of the reasons I got involved with OneWorld was that chance encounter with Paul Cayard, one of the real top American professional sailors of his era, whom I had come across on holiday in the British Virgin Islands. His viewpoint was that if you are going to get involved in any sailing team, sign up with one which is well funded, professionally run and has a potentially successful feel about it. That made quite a big impression on me.

These days, I am often asked to offer advice to young people myself – on what it takes to be a winner. What I try to impress upon them, more than anything, is to watch and listen: learn from the people around you; from the top guys at the local sailing club, the people teaching you, the coaches. *But*, also, don't just learn from what people are doing well, but from what they are *not* doing well, and try to avoid those pitfalls yourself.

And most important of all, enjoy your sailing. If you don't, it's unlikely that you'll be successful anyway. You have to be passionate about it to do well.

There was no doubting that in my own character. I look back at how intense I was when I was younger. I was a real mercurial character: very shy off the water but liable to be incredibly fiery on it. I was aggressive a couple of times when I didn't need to be. I was rude to people when I should have had a bit more respect. But that was my way of dealing with particular issues then. Maybe I should have relaxed more but perhaps that intensity drove me on to work harder.

I'm one of those people who tries to analyse things, and develop, and be a better person. I'm still working at it. You never really know what people think about you, and how you're regarded. I hope it's good overall, though that's not always easy when you're in the public eye.

I guess I've always been pretty ruthless when it comes to competition. I completely differentiate between when I'm racing and everything that goes on after the event. It's about racing, and racing to win. I am galvanised by the mere prospect of a classic confrontation, like that duel with Robert Scheidt at Sydney . . . a battle in which it was all about the encounter. Not the money, or sponsors, or anything going on in the background. I used to love watching the Schumacher, Hill and Villeneuve rivalries. It was classic sport. I could totally relate to that. They were so focussed when they were in the car and ready to go. They didn't give a stuff about anything else when they were racing.

Over these two decades, my love for sailing at any level has never diminished. I love being on the water. But competing, and the buzz you get, takes it to a different level. The harder it is, the more pressure there is, and the tougher the competition, then the bigger the kick you get from it. That feeling of being on the edge in a must-win situation produces an incredible focus which I guess most other sportsmen have felt when they are being pushed to the limit.

Sailing in a team, whether in the World Match-Racing Tour or America's Cup boats, we all need to be operating and thinking at the same level. We must all respect our fellow crew members. It would be impossible for me to sail in the same manner that I go about things in a single-handed boat. With a team it's all about communicating well and working together to be successful.

Whatever the competition, you have to seek perfection. I demand of myself that I make the right decisions. If I don't, I'm not happy. The frustration is still as great as it's always been. You've got to hate losing.

So, what about the future?

As I've said, I would like to put something back into a sport which has done so much for me. I am a director of the National Sailing Academy, and it would be nice to dedicate some more time to that as well as help the sport continue in the right direction, building a profile as one of the most successful of British sports.

I'd also like to do more charity work. I am an ambassador of the Prince's Trust which does so much for young children around the country. And I am also involved with the John Merricks Sailing Trust which raises money to help talented youngsters – people like John himself, who didn't have much financial support when he started out. A wealthy guy at his local club bought him his first boat, and supported him through the beginning of his sailing career. The Trust provides grants to go to an event, or buy a boat.

But I don't expect to be a guy in a blazer when the next Olympics come around. Although to an extent everything hinges on how the America's Cup wrangle resolves itself, my intention is to be here, and qualify for the London Games. I'll have a lot of work to do to get in shape for them. As I've emphasised already, with each Olympics, greater fitness is required. By the summer of 2012, I'll be in my mid-30s, so it'll be even more important. But the intervening months do give me a chance to contemplate other challenges.

Match-racing is an integral part of America's Cup racing and so I will continue to compete on the World Match-Racing Tour. The tour is great for us to go out and hone our skills in this area which is so important to the America's Cup. The boats are very different to the America's Cup boats, being about half the size, but the match-racing principles are the same and we are beginning to build some good relationships. We won't make enough events to challenge for the top of the tour but perhaps that is something for the future.

As I complete this book I have just participated in the Transpac Race from Los Angeles to Hawaii, with Neville Crichton. In doing so, we beat the race record by over a day. At Christmas, I am planning to do the Sydney to Hobart race again, with Neville. My much longer-term future may also include more long-distance ocean racing. There is the Volvo Ocean Race to consider, which would be particularly poignant as my father competed in the first, when it was the Whitbread.

Times have certainly changed greatly since then. In his ocean-racing days, financial rewards did not exist. 'We were scratching to find money to keep the boat afloat the whole way round,' he recalled in a *Sunday Times* article. 'None of the crew were paid and I certainly didn't earn a penny out of it. It took years to pay back what it cost me.'

Today, we are fortunate that major sponsors want to be associated with the sport. However, the race itself, 37,000 nautical miles through some of the world's most perilous seas, is no less demanding of a sailor's nerve or courage.

Another ambition of mine is to compete for the Jules Verne trophy which is for the fastest circumnavigation of the globe by a sailing vessel. The current record is held by Frenchman Bruno Peyron and his team who set a new record of 50 days, 16 hours, 20 minutes and 4 seconds in their giant 36m catamaran *Orange II*. There are many records in the world of sailing but for me this, as well as the transatlantic one, has the greatest aura and attraction. Sailing is a fantastic sport because of its diversity and inclusiveness. As a racing sailor, though, there is always the temptation to chase trophies and records and this is something of which I am wary.

My belief is that if you are going to compete in a race or competition then you need to be properly prepared and you need to give yourself the best possible chance of being successful. Too many times you can be talked into a race where you aren't prepared and it frustrates the hell out of you when you then go on to put in a poor performance. Losing is fine when you've given absolutely everything to the cause, but when you know that you've been put in an impossible position, that's when it becomes difficult.

But that won't deter me from seeking new challenges and trying to push myself forward. I will never stop learning, and in a perfect world, I will fulfil myself as a complete yachtsman.

That's still a long way off – though, speaking of a perfect world, so far, it's just about been that since it all began for me, as a young boy, one special Christmas morning down in Cornwall.

And despite sailing close to the wind on occasions . . .

Glossary

'720' 132
A 720 degree penalty turn or two circles including two tacks and two gybes. This is taken as a penalty to exonerate a boat from a rule infringement that may have occurred.

afterguard 113
The afterguard is a term used in big-boat racing where the sailors at the back of the boat, primarily the helmsman, tactician and navigator, are making the key decisions on strategy and manoeuvring.

backstay 116
A key part of the yacht's rigging which is used to control the bend characteristics of the mast.

bear away / bore away 4
To alter course away from the wind.

beat 44
Sailing as close to the wind as possible on a zigzag course with frequent tacks.

bowsprit 147
A pole projecting from the bow of the boat which is used to fly the downwind spinnaker or gennaker.

discard 2
In most series competitors are allowed to drop their worst race score from the overall series.

foil 123
A collective term for the keel, centreboard (or daggerboard), and rudder.

forestay 143
The forestay is another crucial part of the rigging to hold the mast in place but it is also used to fly the headsail from.

gybe / gybed 5
When the boat alters course whilst sailing downwind, causing the wind to blow on to the boat from a different direction and causing the mainsail to switch sides.

hiking strap 4
A strap used to support the body in extending outside of the boat to create more righting moment.

jib 118
Also called the headsail, this is the front sail used for sailing upwind.

ketch 13
A two-masted sailing yacht.

luff / luffed 4
A boat in control can luff a boat closer to the wind and force her to keep clear. To luff up is to sail closer to the wind.

mainsheet 12
The rope used to control the mainsail.

pitch-poled 150
Turning the boat upside down with the bow nose-diving under the water.

port tack 65
With the wind on the left-hand side. A boat on port tack usually has to give way to a boat on starboard tack.

protest / protested 4
Bringing an incident to the attention of a jury who will hear a case and make a decision to penalise a competitor or not.

pulpit 143
A metal rail around the bow of a boat.

reach 88
Sailing with the wind approximately at right angles to the boat.

reef / reefed 231
To reduce sail area by partly lowering or furling the sail.

sheets 74
The ropes that control the sails.

spinnaker 118
The downwind sail hoisted to give more sail area and speed.

starboard tack 65
With the wind on the right-hand side. A boat on starboard tack usually has right of way over a boat on port tack.

tack 4
Changing direction whilst sailing upwind, causing the mainsail to switch sides.

trapeze 150
A wire used to suspend a crewman outside of the boat and create more righting moment.

trim 12
To adjust the sails to the angle of the wind, creating more speed.

yawl 17
A twin-masted sailing boat where the boom of the aft mast extends past the stern of the boat.

List of Achievements

Competitive Sailing

Career details
1988–1992 – Optimist class
1992–1993 – Laser Radial class
1993–2000 – Team GB, Olympic Laser class
2000–2001 – OneWorld America's Cup challenge
2001 to date – Team GB, Olympic Finn class
2004 to 2007 – Emirates Team New Zealand America's Cup challenge
2007 – Named as Skipper for TeamOrigin (British America's Cup challenge)

Olympic medals
1996 – SILVER Olympics Laser class, Atlanta
2000 – GOLD Olympics Laser class, Sydney
2004 – GOLD Olympics Finn class, Athens
2008 – GOLD Olympics Finn class, Beijing

World Titles
1993 – GOLD Laser Radial world championships
1995 – GOLD ISAF Youth world championships (Laser class)
1998 – GOLD Laser world championships
1999 – GOLD Laser world championships
2002 – GOLD Finn world championships
2003 – GOLD Finn world championships

2004 – GOLD Finn world championships

2005 – GOLD Finn world championships

2006 – GOLD Finn class Pre-Olympic Test Event, Qingdao, China

2006 – 1st Maxi Yacht Rolex Cup (Racing Division) *Shockwave*

2008 – GOLD Finn World Championships

European Titles

1993 – GOLD Laser Radial European championships

1996 – GOLD Laser European championships

1998 – GOLD Laser European championships

1999 – GOLD Laser European championships

2000 – GOLD Laser European championships

2002 – GOLD Finn European championships

2003 – GOLD Finn European championships

2005 – GOLD Finn European championships

2008 – GOLD Finn European championships

Youth Titles

1992 – 1st UK Optimist national championships

1994 – SILVER ISAF Youth world championships

1995 – GOLD ISAF Youth world championships (Laser class)

1995 – 1st RYA British Olympic Trials (Laser class)

World Match-Racing Tour Results

2005 – 2nd PT Portugal Match Cup

2005 – 5th St Moritz Match Race

2008 – 3rd Bermuda Gold Cup

2009 – 1st Germany Match Cup

2009 – 3rd Korea Match Cup

Offshore Results

2001 – 2nd One Ton Cup

2001 – 1720 European champion

2003 – 3rd Admirals Cup IMS class

2005 – 4th Middle Sea Race *Aera*

Other Results
2008 – 1st Etchell Australian championships

Honours

2001 – MBE
2005 – OBE
2008 – CBE

Awards

1995 – British Young Sailor of the Year
1996 – Sports Writers' Association Best International Newcomer
1998 – International Sailing Federation World Sailor of the Year
2002 – International Sailing Federation World Sailor of the Year
2004 – BBC South Sports Awards: Best Yachtsperson
2004 – Induction into the Finn Hall of Fame
2004 – BBC South Sports Awards: Yachtsman of the year
2005 – BBC South Sports Awards: Best Sportsman
2008 – British Olympic Association Athlete of the Year for Sailing
2008 – BBC Southwest Yachtsman of the year
2008 – International Sailing Federation World Sailor of the Year
2008 – BBC South Sports Awards: Yachtsman of the year
2008 – BBC South Sports Awards: Sports Personality of the year
Also named Raymarine/YJA British Yachtsman of the Year on five
occasions: 2008, 2004, 2002, 2000 & 1999

Honorary Doctor of Sport, Southampton University
Honorary Doctorate in Law, Exeter University
Honorary Degree in Sport Science, University College of Chichester

Honorary member Royal Cornwall Yacht Club
Honorary member Stokes Bay Sailing Club
Honorary member Restronguet Sailing Club
Honorary member Hayling Island Sailing Club
Honorary member Royal Lymington Yacht Club

Acknowledgements

To Jo Grindley and everyone at 'Into the blue' for convincing me to do this book and try to help people understand what the sport of sailing is all about.

To Nick Townsend for his patience and dealing with many weird time zones whilst trying to put this book together.

To everyone at Random House and Yellow Jersey for all their help and efforts. Especially Tristan Jones and Rowan Yapp.

To Phil Slater for teaching me how to sail in the first place.

To the Royal Yachting Association for their support over the years.

To all my sponsors who have been so supportive and helped me get to the startline.

To Mel Coleman for always making me realise how lucky I am to be able to go sailing as a career.

To my parents, my sister Fleur, her husband Jerome, my niece and nephew Tansy and Oscar for all their support and for always being there.